THE SPEYS

A History and Guide
to the Railway from
Craigellachie to Boat of Garten

A Speyside train waits to leave Craigellachie in very early LNER days. The locomotive is class M No.57, which was withdrawn in 1925, while the coaches are still in GNSR two-colour livery. Elderly locomotives were often used on the Speyside line. (Sir Malcolm Barclay-Harvey/GNSRA collection)

Dick Jackson and Keith Fenwick

Great North of Scotland Railway Association
January 2012

The 2.55pm down train for Boat of Garten has just left Dailuaine Halt on 25th September 1956 headed by No.62271, one of the GNSR Class V (NER Class D40). The overbridge carries the drive to Carron House while the connection to Dailuaine Distillery is a short distance behind the photographer.   (J L Stevenson)

Contents

Front cover : A special train from Invernes to Aberdeen via Aviemorein June 1962 hauled by No.49 'Gordon Highlander' and Highland Railway No.103 provided a last opportunity to travel behind a Great North 4-4-0 on Speyside, a type which will be forever associated with the line. It is seen here at Ballindalloch where it stopped for photographs.   (Norris Forrest/GNSRA)

What could be better than a leisurely trip along Speyside in sunny weather. The crew of D8032 must have enjoyed their journey on the 2pm goods as it leaves Craigellachie for Aviemore on 23rd June 1966. The map shows this part of the river as 'Nook Water or Cairn Pool'.   (Colour-Rail.com, ref 214875).

Introduction

The Spey ranks as one of the great rivers of Scotland. Over 100 miles separate its source high in the mountains to the west of Aviemore and its mouth on the Moray Firth but being fast flowing and shallow it is unsuitable for navigation. Despite that it was for very many years an important transport artery as floating proved the simplest way of moving timber harvested along its banks. To-day most people will connect it with whisky and the sport provided by that king of fish, the salmon.

Over 150 years ago a writer said of its middle reaches that "nature has forced her to thread her course around the bases of mountains and often for miles together she is confined by precipitous banks on both sides, in many cases so steep that on looking at them a spectator would pronounce a railway along them impossible." However a railway was indeed built beside the river from Craigellachie to Boat of Garten and that forms the subject of this book.

Strathspey is very scenic, particularly between Grantown and Craigellachie, but the river itself is somewhat secretive so that the present day traveller on the main road between these towns sees little of it. Time was when the best way to enjoy this picturesque journey was by train. The railway was never very far from the river, indeed there were places where the track seemed almost to hang above the water. Altogether it was a truly delightful journey.

The trains were never in a hurry and while this may have pleased the visitor, for the local people it could be a different matter. Inevitably the increasing use of cars and lorries meant less traffic for the railway so that the passenger service ended in October 1965 and the line closed completely a few years later. Fortunately today those with time to spare can walk or cycle much of the route between Craigellachie and Nethy Bridge as it is incorporated in the Speyside Way and tourists on the modern Strathspey Railway from Aviemore to Broomhill can enjoy the scenery and travel over the southern end of the Strathspey line where it shared tracks with the Highland Railway.

This book first appeared as *The Speyside Line* in 1996 and a second edition followed ten years later, both written by Dick Jackson. Dick is no longer with us, so this revised edition has been produced by his friends in the Great North of Scotland Railway Association.

New material has been added to enhance the history of the line and some topics which were previously described in separate headings have been woven into the main story. The changes in the line's fortunes in the 1950s and early 1960s have received more attention. The description of the line has been greatly expanded and related to what you can see today. Even since the publication of the earlier editions of this book, changes have taken place and these are incorporated.

Thanks go to Mrs Elizabeth Jackson for permission to use her husband's text and to everyone else who has contributed. Photographers are acknowledged in the captions; other photographs are from the Association's collection. OS maps are reproduced with kind permission of the Trustees of the National Library of Scotland.

Keith Fenwick
January 2012

Unlike many rural branch lines, the Speyside line had junctions at each end. At Craigellachie, above, where a southbound train is waiting to leave in the early 1950s, connection was made with the Great North main line from Keith to Elgin via Dufftown. At Boat of Garten, seen below in LNER days with a mixed train arriving, the Speyside line connected with the original Highland main line from Perth to Inverness via Dava. Both trains are hauled by Great North 4-4-0s, D40 No.62268 above and D38 No.6875 below.

(Neville Stead collection, above, and Keith Fenwick collection below)

Early Railways in the Area

The railway between Craigellachie and Boat of Garten was built by the Strathspey Railway Company but this was only one of a number of companies involved in connecting the district with the outside world.

Railway development started in the mid-1840s. Rival schemes were proposed to run between Aberdeen and Inverness, but it was the Great North of Scotland Railway which obtained its Parliamentary Act in 1846 for a line via Keith and Elgin, plus several branches. Two other branches were promoted by the Morayshire Railway which was also authorised by Parliament in 1846; one ran from Elgin to Lossiemouth and the other from Orton to Rothes and the upper Spey. The terminus finally selected for the southern branch was on the west bank of the Spey. It was named Craigellachie, later changed to Dandaleith; to avoid confusion the latter name will be used. The Morayshire would have running powers over the GNSR between Orton and Elgin, a distance of some nine miles. The section from Lossiemouth to Elgin was opened in 1852 before any of the other lines, making it the earliest railway in northern Scotland.

In the event the Great North could not raise the required capital for its project and had to be content with going only as far as Keith, which was reached in October 1856. The route was completed by the Inverness & Aberdeen Junction Railway (later to become part of the Highland Railway) which was opened in sections, concluding on 18th August 1858 when services started between Keith and Elgin. The Morayshire opened its line from Orton to Rothes five days later, reaching Dandalieth on 24th December that year.

All might have been well if the companies had retained friendly relations, but this was not the case. Morayshire engines quickly proved that they were incapable of tackling the gradients of the Inverness company's line, so that latter insisted on working all the trains to avoid serious delays; there were also constant squabbles about train times and payments due. Matters went from bad to worse, so much so that two years later the Morayshire obtained powers to build its own direct line from Elgin to Rothes via Longmorn and this line opened in January 1862.

In the mid-1850s, a branch was promoted between Keith and Dufftown, but this struggled for some time to raise finance. Only when the GNSR became involved did this scheme proceed, construction starting in 1860. The terminus at Dufftown was to be near Little Tulloch, east of the River Fiddich.

By 1860, relations between the Great North of Scotland and Inverness & Aberdeen Junction Railways had reached such a low level that the latter looked again at the proposal to build a direct line from the Inverness area to Perth. This had been put forward in 1845 but was rejected at that time by Parliament because of the gradients involved. A direct line south from Inverness would damage the Great North by taking away its through traffic. This renewed threat was discussed by the Great North directors in 1860 when they instructed their Traffic and Finance Committee to inspect the country and consider its possibilities. In June the Committee reported that a line down Speyside from Dufftown to Abernethy (later called Nethy Bridge) would benefit the district and they were much impressed by the prospect of timber traffic from the large forests in the Grantown area where Lord Seafield alone owned over 41,000 acres, although the Great North failed to appreciate that Seafield was a strong supporter of the Inverness line. Following this, Alexander Gibb, the Company's engineer, was told to make a trial survey.

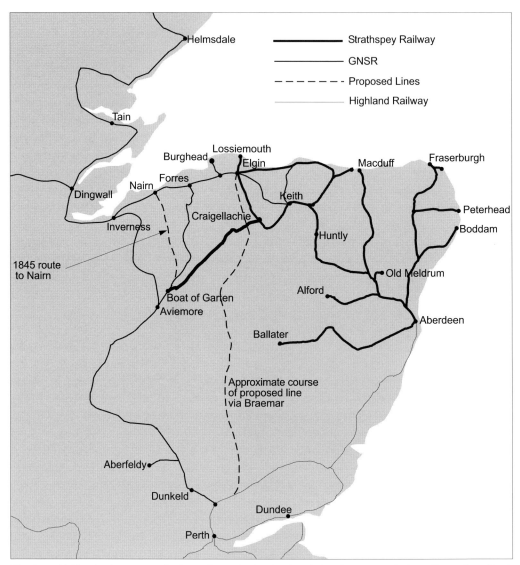

The Speyside line in the context of other railways in Scotland and the other proposals for railways from Perth to Inverness and Elgin.

A Speyside goods train pulls away from Boat of Garten in the early 1900s. The engine appears to be one of three Class C 4-4-0s built in 1878/79 which is shown here as rebuilt. The Highland tracks are in the foreground. (Sir C M Barlcay-Harvey/GNSRA)

Gibb's report refers to three proposed railways, all intended to connect Inverness with Perth, which would to some extent affect a Great North line in the Spey valley. Two of them headed south from the Inverness to Aberdeen route, one from Nairn and the other from Forres. The first of these was abortive but the second, which ran via Grantown and Kingussie, became the Inverness & Perth Junction Railway, later part of the Highland Railway.

The third was an extraordinary suggestion put forward by the little Morayshire Railway, which obviously had big ideas, for a "more direct route" from Elgin. This would have run through Rothes to Ballindalloch and thence via Tomintoul, Braemar, Spital of Glenshee and Blairgowrie. The Morayshire had a survey done by its own engineer and went so far as to send details of this to railway companies "in the south." These admitted the importance of the line and felt it was decidedly preferable to the more circuitous route through Kingussie but hesitated to become involved at that time. Gibb reported that it had severe gradients with a summit tunnel of at least six miles and so he discounted it.

Not long after this comes the first reference to possible traffic from the Duke of Richmond's iron ore mines near Tomintoul. As will be seen later (p75), this was to keep reappearing.

By October 1860 the Great North's new line was officially called the Strathspey Railway and towards the end of year the necessary Bill was laid before Parliament to extend the Keith & Dufftown Railway to a more useful station for Dufftown at Balvenie and then build the Strathspey Railway from there via Craigellachie to Abernethy. The Bill also allowed for the construction of a branch line from Ballifurth, two miles north of Abernethy, to meet the Inverness & Perth Junction Railway at Dulnain Bridge or at an independent terminus, but this was never built. The Bill had an easy passage through Parliament as the Great North and the Inverness & Perth Junction had agreed not to oppose each other. The Bill received Royal Assent in May 1861 on the same date as that for the Inverness & Perth Junction. At the same time the Morayshire received Parliamentary approval to extend its line across the river at Craigellachie from the original terminus to a junction with the Strathspey Railway. This resulted from negotiations with the Great North by which the latter would work the Morayshire and invest in the company.

The Keith & Dufftown Railway opened on 21st February 1862, including the section authorised as part of the Strathspey Railway Act to the station at Balvenie.

THE SPEY VALLEY, BALLINDALLOCH

Typical of the scenery in the upper Spey Valley is this view of Ballindalloch looking north east. The line from Boat of Garten comes in on the left and then swings over the River Spey on its way to Craigellachie. This is one of the wider areas of the valley where construction of the line was easier. Most of the development here came after the railway arrived; before then it was sparsely populated.   (Graham Maxtone collecton)

The final train on the Speyside line, in November 1968, approaches the third crossing of the Spey just south of Nethy Bridge. At this location, the river was narrower so a more modest bridge sufficed compared with the other two along the line.   (Mike Yeoman/GNSRA)

Building the Line

Six months after the Act was passed the tender for the construction of the railway was awarded to Mr Preston of Elgin for the sum of £82,000, the cheapest tender by about £5,000. Construction included two major crossings over the Spey, at Carron and Ballindalloch, which were contracted for separately. Alternative solutions were considered for both of them. At Carron, an iron lattice bridge was suggested but a segmented arch chosen as the river bed is rock and a centre support could not be properly anchored. This cost £3,277. At Ballindalloch, it was possible to cross the river with one lattice span which was supplied by McFarlane of Dundee for £4,800. It was desirable to avoid centre piers as winter floods and floating timber posed a risk of damage. Expert advice was obtained in both cases to ensure that the designs were sound, which indeed turned out to be the case as they survive today, one of them carrying a road. Several road bridges were required where roads had to be realigned to pass over or under the new line.

The *Banffshire Journal* of 29th April 1862 carried an optimistic report of progress on the line; little short of 1000 navvies were employed and working vigorously on the section as far as Carron. Operations had also commenced at Blacksboat. The navvies were reported to have conducted themselves very well "and it may be seen that, at the meeting of the Synod of Moray on Tuesday last, testimony to their excellent behaviour was borne by the minister of Aberlour." However, later that year, the Board was concerned that progress was not as fast as expected. Preston was having difficulty in providing enough men. By October his health had broken and he was unable to continue so the contract was relet.

The positions of the various stations were decided when the directors and officials visited the line in July 1862, although construction of Blacksboat was delayed while the possibility of building a bridge over the river there was considered. Station costs varied between £220 and £275 each.

Money, as always, was tight and it was difficult to keep within the Parliamentary estimate. A wooden engine shed at Abernethy was considered in place of the stone one contracted for, but there is no evidence that this was changed. It was also decided to use second hand rails for the last 5 miles to Abernethy. Again cheapest was not best because when the line was inspected by Colonel Yolland on behalf of the Board of Trade he refused to accept them on the grounds that it would be setting a bad precedent. The Company promised to replace the rails within two months and in the meantime to restrict the speed of trains to 10 mph, and that satisfied the Board of Trade. The Inspecting Officer commented that it was a "line of steep gradients and very sharp curves .... and will in consequence require to be very carefully worked and at a low rate of speed."

The directors and official guests travelled along the line to Abernethy on 25th June 1863 where, on arrival, they sat down to a "sumptuous lunch…..in the large new engine house." Following this the line was opened for traffic on 1st July 1863, with stations at Aberlour, Cromdale, Blacksboat, Ballindalloch, Advie, Dalvey, Cromdale and Grantown.

On the same day the Morayshire opened its extension across the River Spey from Dandaleith to Strathspey Junction, as it was originally called. It did not get its better known name of Craigellachie until 1st June 1864. The Great North was now physically linked to the Morayhsire, giving the former its own route to Elgin and also triggering its undertaking to work the smaller company's traffic. The Rothes to Orton section now served little purpose so it was closed in 1866 to through traffic, much to the annoyance of the Highland. Goods traffic was worked as required until about 1880 although the track remained until 1908.

The Inverness & Perth opened between Aviemore and Forres on 3rd August that year and the line through to Perth on 9th September, so the Grantown area suddenly found itself with two separate railway lines.

To-day it is almost impossible to realise the impact made by the arrival of the railway on a rural area such as Speyside. Until then most people had to walk and goods moved slowly by lumbering wagon over very indifferent roads. Suddenly journeys which had taken days could be made in a matter of hours. When on 18th June 1863 a train carrying Company officials finally ran from Dufftown to Abernethy it is small wonder that the Aberlour correspondent of the *Elgin Courant* waxed ungrammatically lyrical. "All the world knows that a nation's history is made up of events which take place from time to time during revolving ages. In like manner all the readers of the Elgin Courant may now know that an era in the future history of Strathspey dawned on Thursday last which all the world may hear of after the present generation has gone to their last resting place."

Plans for the extension of the Strathspey Railway for 4¾ miles from Abernethy to Boat of Garten, where the Inverness & Perth Junction Railway's station was to be used, were considered in November 1864 but doubts were soon raised as to the wisdom of this. It was felt that the Great North's share of the traffic going south from Speyside would in future travel by the shorter route instead of via Keith and Aberdeen. When it was pointed out that the Strathspey line was an accomplished fact and that somebody else could well move in to fill the gap it was agreed to go ahead. This desire to encourage traffic to go south the long way round via Aberdeen could still be seen seventy years later — the LNER had a large notice at Boat of Garten advertising trains to the south via Aberdeen!

The Strathspey met the Highland Railway at Tullochgorum, not far south of the latter's Broomhill station, but it was not a junction in the accepted sense. As the Highland had no operational

Carron was typical of the station buildings erected along the line for the opening of the Strathspey Railway; simple stone structures with a booking hall in the centre, station offices on one end and ladies waiting room at the other. By the 1960s little had changed except for the wooden screen in the centre which was a later addition; this area of the building was originally open to the elements.   *(GNSRA collection)*

need for a signal box there it laid a second track parallel to its own for the final three miles to 'The Boat' for the exclusive use of Speyside trains. The actual junction between the two Companies was originally at the south end of the station although another connection was installed at the north end in 1907.

Early in July 1866 an engine was taken through to Boat of Garten and opening was confidently expected on the 21st of the month. However the Board of Trade inspector, Captain Tyler, asked for some further work to be done on the bridge crossing the Spey and for alterations to the signalling between Abernethy and Boat of Garten. These were not serious matters and trains started running on 1st August. On the same day the Keith & Dufftown and Strathspey Railways were formally incorporated into the Great North of Scotland Railway.

Also on 1st August the Inverness & Aberdeen Junction and the Inverness & Perth Junction Railways amalgamated to form the Highland Railway. With the opening to Boat of Garten, the Great North could exchange traffic with the Highland not only there but also at Elgin and

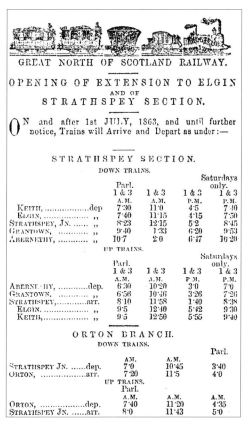

GREAT NORTH OF SCOTLAND RAILWAY.

OPENING OF EXTENSION TO ELGIN
AND OF
STRATHSPEY SECTION.

ON and after 1st JULY, 1863, and until further notice, Trains will Arrive and Depart as under :—

STRATHSPEY SECTION.
DOWN TRAINS.

	Parl. 1 & 3	1 & 3	1 & 3	Saturdays only. 1 & 3
	A.M.	A.M.	P.M.	P.M.
KEITH, ... dep	7·30	11·0	4·5	7·40
ELGIN, ... ,,	7·40	11·15	4·15	7·50
STRATHSPEY, JN. ...... ,,	8·23	12·15	5·2	8·45
GRANTOWN, ... ,,	9·40	1·33	6·20	9·53
ABERNETHY, ... ,,	10·7	2·0	6·47	10·20

UP TRAINS.

	Parl. 1 & 3	1 & 3	1 & 3	Saturdays only. 1 & 3
	A.M.	A.M.	P.M.	P.M.
ABERNETHY, ... dep.	6·30	10·20	3·0	7·0
GRANTOWN. .... ,,	6·56	10·36	3·26	7·26
STRATHSPEY, ... arr.	8·10	11·58	1·40	8·38
ELGIN. .... ,,	9·5	12·40	5·42	9·30
KEITH, ... ,,	9·5	12·50	5·55	9·40

ORTON BRANCH.
DOWN TRAINS.

			Parl.
	A.M.	A.M.	
STRATHSPEY JN. ......dep.	7·0	10·45	3·40
ORTON, ... arr.	7·20	11·5	4·0

UP TRAINS.

	Parl.		
	A.M.	A.M.	A.M.
ORTON, ... dep.	7·40	11·20	4·35
STRATHSPEY JN. ......arr.	8·0	11·43	5·0

Keith, a situation which was to cause endless problems and almost war-like relations for many years. Indeed it was not until the turn of the century that anything like normal co-operation existed between them. This attitude led to problems when it came to agreeing the rent to be paid for the use of Boat of Garten station and the track out as far as Tullochgorum. The Great North contended that it should only pay interest on the cost of the second track and a small part of the cost of the station. The Highland wanted interest on the total cost including the station work. The dispute was eventually resolved by an Arbiter appointed by the Board of Trade and resulted in the GNSR paying £854 per annum, a figure which remained unaltered at least until 1910 when the amount was no longer itemised in the accounts.

The Spey presented an obstacle to serving both side of the valley by a railway which ran down one side. Some places were only served by ferries across the river. This suspension footbridge at Cromdale was built in 1881 to replace the ferry there and was in turn replaced by the present road bridge in the late 1920s.

(John Diffey collection)

A typical Great North Speyside train headed by Class M No.57 approaches Boat of Garten on the double track section. Although taken in early LNER days, the engine still carries its original number and some of the coaches are in Great North livery. The coaches are all 6 wheelers and consist of a full brake, a composite with centre luggage compartment and two thirds. This was the standard formation of trains at that time.

(GNSRA collection)

Carron station, as seen from Imperial Distillery, in the early years of the 20th century. The goods yard is on the far side of the station towards the trees. The sidings in the foreground served the distillery. The developing whisky industry was an important source of traffic on the Speyside line, although no other distilleries were as large as Imperial.

(Ross Kerby collection/GNSRA)

Slow Development

Despite the usual optimism which had attended the promotion of the line, traffic was very limited at first. In the middle of the nineteenth century, the Spey Valley was fairly sparsely inhabited. There were a few whisky distilleries but otherwise the area was purely agricultural.

Trains on the line were never numerous or speedy. The first timetable, for July 1863, showed three trains each way with an extra return journey on Saturday evenings. In connection with the first Up, northbound, train a coach left Tomintoul at 4.30am for Ballindalloch returning after the arrival of the last Down train. The first train in each direction was the statutory Parliamentary which had to stop at all stations (in fact every train did so) at a fare of 1d per mile as against the standard 1½d paid by Third Class passengers and 2d by those in First Class. To say the trains were slow is an understatement; most averaged 16½ mph while the Up Parliamentary barely achieved 11mph.

When the extension to Boat of Garten opened on 1st August 1866 the service consisted of two 'mixed' (i.e. passenger coaches plus goods wagons) and two passenger trains northbound and one passenger and two mixed trains southbound, the engine workings being balanced by a goods train. The mixed trains took an average of 1 hour 40 minutes for the 33½ miles while the passenger trains required about twenty minutes less. This standard of service must have proved excessive as it was not long before there were only two mixed trains each way with a third added for the summer months only. However as traffic increased three return journeys became the standard pattern. A survey of branch line costs and revenue in 1871 showed that the line was covering its working costs, but there was little left over to pay a return on the capital.

One of the incentives to build the railway was the existence of large areas of forest in the district. As early as October 1865 one of the GNSR directors met Mr Grant of Rothiemurchus regarding the transport of timber from Aviemore to Aberdeen for which a rate not exceeding 1d per ton per mile was quoted. Two years later a siding was authorised at Pollowick, about 1½ miles north of Cromdale, for use in moving timber from Lord Seafield's estate, almost all of which was going to Glasgow via Aberdeen.

Over the next 30 years, revenue improved slowly, helped by the growth in the whisky industry. Speyside is almost synonymous with whisky, but did whisky bring the railway or was it vice versa? In truth there was probably a little bit of both. Licensing of distilleries began in 1824 and, so far as those in a position to use the Speyside line are concerned, among the first to be granted were Balmenach, Cardhu and The Glenlivet (all 1824), Aberlour (1826), followed by Glenfarclas (1836) and Dailuaine (1852). Once the railway had arrived other distilleries were built close to it. Cragganmore, opened in 1869, was the first followed by Tamdhu (1896), Imperial in 1897 and then Knockando the following year.

STRATHSPEY SECTION.			
DOWN TRAINS.			
Parl.			
	A.M.	A.M.	P.M.
KEITH, ...dep.	7·20	9·50	4·5	—
ELGIN, ... ,,	7·30	10·10	4·20	—
CRAIGELLACHIE JUN. .,	8·10	10·45	5·15	—
GRANTOWN, ... ,,	9·24	11·40	6·41	—
BOAT OF GARTEN,.... arr.	9·45	12·7P	7·5	—
Do. N.B.,........	—	6·20	—	—
EDINBURGH, CAL.,.........	—	7·0	—	—
GLASGOW, ...	—	6·15	—	—
LONDON (L. & N.W.).....	—	4·37A	—	—
Do. (G. N.), ...	—	9·40	—	—
UP TRAINS.			
	A.M.	A.M.	P.M.
LONDON(L. & N.W.)...dep.	10·0	8·40	9·15	—
Do. (G.N.), ...	10·0	10·0A	9·15	—
GLASGOW, ...	9·0P	6·40	9·35A	—
EDINBURGH, CAL.,.........	8·45	6·40	9·15	—
Do. (N. B.), ...	6·45	6·25	9·45	—
Parl.			
	A.M.	A.M.	P.M.	P.M.
BOAT OF GARTEN JN.,....dep.	6·10	10·10	12·50	5·5
GRANTOWN, ... ,,	6·37	10·32	1·11	5·25
CRAIGELLACHIE,......... ,,	8·17	12·0	2·10	6·33
ELGIN, ... ,,	7·30	11·10	—	5·45
KEITH, ... ,,	9·0	12·45	3·0	7·15

1866 timetable — the first to Boat of Garten.

The railways played an integral part in the delivery of mail until the latter part of the twentieth century. With few other facilities in rural areas, many stations acted as the local post office. Railways also needed their own telegraph links and, to help offset the cost of installing them, these were made available to the Post Office for public use, further integrating the work of the Post Office and the  local railway station. The Post Office paid generously for these services but in return enforced strict contractual conditions which included, in some cases, specific train times and speeds.

Post Office distribution was based on mail being taken to the nearest post town for sorting. If not for local delivery, it could then only be sent to another post town for further sorting and final delivery. On Speyside, the post towns were Craigellachie and Grantown but it was inefficient to send mail between addresses served by the same station to the post town for sorting. So the mail was sorted at the stations, which were designated as Railway Suboffices. This scheme came to an end on 1st July 1905, when many of the stations became independent suboffices, this arrangement continuing into LNER days and in some instances until the line closed to passenger traffic in 1965. Station names appeared on the stamp used to frank outgoing mail.

Improvements were gradually made to the facilities on the line and to the track and signalling. Steel rails replaced iron towards the end of the 19th century. In 1889, new government rules required that all points and signals be interlocked and that block signalling be introduced. The Great North adopted the tablet system for ensuring that only one train was allowed into each block section at a time and this became operational on the Speyside line in 1894. New signalling was installed at Ballindalloch in 1892, and Carron and Grantown in 1894. In 1896, a siding was opened to serve Tamdhu distillery; a public station, known as Dalbeallie, was opened there in 1899 to serve the district but this is better known as Knockando, the name adopted in 1905. To cope with the increasing traffic, new passing places were installed at Cromdale in 1907 and Aberlour in 1910.

By the 1890s, there were still three through trains each way, but in addition a couple of mixed trains from Craigellachie to Ballindalloch and back. The service was further expanded a few years later when a separate goods train was run the whole length of the line, plus one as far as Ballindalloch only and another to and from Tamdhu and another to Carron, making nine in all from Craigellachie. Of the three trains over the whole length of the line, only one was mixed and the mail train managed the journey in 65 minutes. The peak was reached in the summer of 1914 as shown in the timetable opposite.

The line carried additional traffic from about 1906 as a result of greater cooperation between the Great North and Highland. The Great North

After 1889, railways were required to interlock points and signals and to introduce block signalling. As a result, signal boxes were erected at all the crossing points. The box at Carron was a typical Great North design of the period, simple and functional. It remained in use until the line closed. (GNSRA)

DOWN TRAINS.

Miles from Craigellachie	STATIONS.	1	2	3	4	5	6	7	8	9	10
		a.m.	a.m.	a.m.		a.m.	p.m.	p.m.	a.m.	p.m.	a.m.
	Aberdeen de.	3‡30	4 35	8 5	......	10 5	1 0	......	10 12	3 40	10 12
	Banff „	......	......	7 20	......	10 55	......	......	......	4 25	......
	Keith „	7 20	7 45	......	......	12 5p	......	......	3 5p	5 40	4 40
	Keith Town „	7 23	......	9 37	......	12 8	......	......	......	5 43	.....
....	Dufftown „	7 46	8 41	9 56	......	12 31	......	......	......	6 7	6 30
....	Lossiemouth de.	......	......	8 25	......	9 45a	.....	2 12	12 15	5 30	3 30
....	Elgin „	7 5	6 15	9 30	......	10 22	Weds. and Sats.	2 40	2 15	5 50	4 50
		Pass. a.m.	Goods a.m.	Mixed. a.m.		Mixed. p.m.	Pass. p.m.	Mail & Pass. p.m.	Goods p.m.	Pass p.m.	Goods. p.m.
....	Craigellachie de.	8 0	9 45	10 15	......	12 45	2 30	3 15	4 15	6 30	7 15
2¼	Aberlour „	8 5	9 57	10 21	......	12 51	2 36	3 20	4 40	6 35	7 27
5⅓	Carron ar.	......	......	......	......	......	......	.....	4 55	......	......
....	Do. de.	8 11	10 13	10 30	......	1 0	2d42	3 26	5 15	6 41	7 43
8	Knockando ar.	......	10 22	......	......	......	......	......	......	......	......
....	Do. de.	8 17	10 57	10 37	*When re-quired Goods a.m.*	1 6	2d47	3 31	5 48	6 46	7 58
10¼	Blacksboat „	8 23	11 7	10 46		1 14	......	3 36	......	6 52	8 8
12	Ballindalloch ar.	8 27	11 13	10 52		1 20	2t53	......	......	......	8 15
....	Ballindalloch de.	......	......	10 56	*11 25*	......	2 55	3 41	6 13	6 57	8¶25
15¼	Advie „	......	......	11 7	......	......	......	3 47	......	7 4	8 35
21	Cromdale „	......	......	11 23	......	......	......	3 57	......	7 14	8 52
24	Grantown-on Spey „	......	......	11 34	*12p5*	......	3 13	4 3	......	7 20	9 5
28¼	Nethy Bridge „	......	......	11 47	......	......	3 22	4 12	......	7 30	9 18
33¼	Boat of Garten ar.	......	......	12 0	*12 25*	......	3 30	4 20	7 5	7 40	9 30
				p.m.				p.m.	p.m.	Goods.	p.m.
....	Boat of Garten de.	......	......	12 28	......	......	......	4 39	7 15	10 30p	11 20
....	Aviemore ar	......	......	12 32	......	......	......	4 48	7 27	10 45	11 35
....	Kingussie „	......	......	12 58	......	......	......	5 14	8 10	......	12 10a
....	Aberfeldy „	......	......	3*10	......	......	......	......	......	......	7 55
....	Dunkeld „	......	......	2*55	......	......	......	......	......	......	8 15
....	Perth „	......	......	3 33	......	......	......	7 12	11 15	2 40a	3 25
....	Dundee „	......	......	4 20	......	......	......	8 50	......	......	......
....	Edin. (v. Forth Br.) „	......	......	5 33	......	......	......	9 17	......	......	......
....	Do. (v. Dunblane and Stirling) „	......	......	5 43	......	......	......	10 4	......	......	......
....	Glasg. (v. AlloaBr.) „	......	......	7 0	......	......	......	10‖8	......	......	......
....	Do. (Buch. St.) „	......	......	5 30	......	......	......	9e30	......	......	......
....	Lond. (Euston) „	......	......	8 50a	......	......	......	7 50a	......	......	......
....	Do. (St. Pancras) „	......	......	5 45	......	......	......	7 35	......	......	......
....	Do. (King's Cr.) „	......	......	5 50	......	......	......	7 10	......	......	......

‖ Does not wait at Perth beyond 7·30 p.m. for Highland Company's Train.

* Stops to set down on notice being given to Guard at Blair-Atholl.

‡ Also leaves Aberdeen at 5·50 a.m. on Mondays only.

¶ 10 minutes later from Ballindalloch to Boat of Garten on Wednesdays and Saturdays.

d Stops for crossing purposes only.

e Glasgow (Central Station).

t Water Engine and snip Tickets.

Strathspey Section — UP TRAINS.

Miles from Garten Junct.	STATIONS.	1	2	3	4	5	6	7	8	9	10	11
		a.m.	a.m.		p.m.		p.m.		a.m.	a.m.		
....	Lond. (King's Cr) de.	10 35	......	......	8†0	......	11‡30	......	......	......	......	......
....	Do. (St. Pancras) „	11 30	......	......	......	......	9‡30	......	......	......	......	......
....	Do. (Euston) „	2 0p	......	......	8†0	......	11‡45	......	......	......	......	......
....	Edin. (v. Forth Br.) „	9 6	......	......	4 0a	......	7 45a	......	......	10 5	......	......
....	Do. (v. Stirling & Dunblane) „	9 45	......	......	4 0	......	7 0	......	......	9 25	......	......
....	Glasg. (v. AlloaBr.) „	7j22	......	......	......	......	6 44	......	......	9 10	......	......
....	Do. (Buch. St.) „	10 0	......	......	4b20	......	7 30	......	......	10 0	......	......
....	Dundee „	10 40	......	......	..	......	8 5	......	......	10 35	......	......
....	Perth „	12§50a	1 0	......	6 15	......	9 30	......	1 30	11 50	......	......
....	Dunkeld „	1§26	......	......	6 10	......	10 4	......	8 25	12c10	......	......
....	Aberfeldy „	......	......	......	......	......	9 40	......	6 45	12c15	......	......
....	Kingussie „	3§28	4 36	......	8 16	......	12 11p	......	5 40	2 29	......	......
....	Aviemore „	4§0	5 10	......	8 40	......	12 50	......	6 20	2'52	......	......
....	Boat of Garten ar.	4§10	5 25	......	8 49	......	12 59	......	6 37	3 0	......	......
		Mixed. a.m.	Goods a.m.	Pass. a.m.	Mail & Pass. a.m.	Goods. a.m.	Mixed p.m.	*When re-quir'd Goods p.m.*	Goods. p.m.	Pass p.m.		Weds and Sats. Pass p.m.
....	Boat of Garten de.	5 30	6 45	......	9 30	......	......	*12 45*	1 5	4 55	......	8 0
4¾	Nethy Bridge „	5 43	......	......	9 39	......	......	......	1 27	5 4	......	8 9
9¼	Grantown-on-Spey „	5 56	7 8	......	9 48	......	......	......	1 50	5 13	......	8 18
12¼	Cromdale ar.	......	......	......	......	......	......	......	......	......	......	......
....	Cromdale de.	6 6	7 19	......	9 54	......	......	......	2 10	5 19	......	......
18	Advie „	6 21	......	......	10 5	......	......	......	2 30	5 30	......	......
21½	Ballindalloch ar.	6 30	7 40	......	......	......	......	*1 45*	2 39	......	......	......
	Do. de.	6 40	7 50	9 14	10 13	11 25	2 15	*1 50*	3 0	5 38	......	8 36
23	Blacksboat „	6 47	.....	9 18	10 17	11 35	2 20	*2 2*	3 15	5 42	......	......
25½	Knockando ar.	......	8 2	......	......	......	......	*2 10*	3 25	......	......	......
....	Do. de.	6 55	8 17	9 24	10 24	11 53	2 27	*2 45*	3 45	5 48	......	......
27¾	Carron „	7 3	8 30	9 30	10 30	12p13	2¶35	*3 8*	4 25	5 53	......	......
31	Aberlour ar.	......	. . .	......	. . .	......	. . .	*3 18*	4 36	......	......	......
....	Do. de.	7 13	8 43	9 38	10 37	12 33	2 44	*3 38*	4 52	6 0	......	8 52
33½	Craigellachie ar.	7 20	8 50	9 43	10 42	12 40	2 50	*3 45*	5 0	6 5	......	8 57
....	Elgin ar.	8 30	10 10	10 34	11 25	......	4 44	......	7 55	6 50	......	......
....	Lossiemouth „	9 27	11 45	10 57	11 45	......	5 7	......	......	7 47	......	......
....	Dufftown „	7 46	9 35	......	11 0	......	3 15	......	5 50	6 29	......	......
....	Keith Town „	8 8	......	......	11 21	......	3 33	......	......	6 52	......	......
....	Keith „	8 11	10 30	......	......	......	......	......	6 43	6 55	......	......
....	Banff „	10 20	......	......	12p45	......	6 15	......	......	8 50	......	......
....	Aberdeen „	9 55	4 54	......	12 50	......	5 10	......	10 25	10d10	......	10 32

b Glasgow Central Station.

c Stops by Signal to lift Passengers for north of Blair-Atholl.

d On Saturdays arrives Aberdeen at 8·53 p.m.

j 8·0 p.m. *via* Forth Bridge.

§ Mondays excepted.

‡ Also runs on Sunday nights.

† Not on Saturdays.

* Saturdays only.

¶ 7 minutes later from Carron to Craigellachie on Wednesdays and Saturdays.

June 1914 working timetable.

had traditionally routed as much through traffic to the south as possible via Aberdeen to maximise the revenue it received. However, taking the two companies together, greater income could be gained by routing this traffic via Perth.

From July 1910, Ballindalloch was connected with Tomintoul by a GNSR motor omnibus running during the summer months only, a service which continued until October 1925.

BETWEEN BALLINDALLOCH AND TOMINTOUL.
This service commences on 30th May.

BALLINDALLOCH TO TOMINTOUL.

By Train.	A.M.	P.M. Weds. & Sats.	A.M.
Aberdeen, dep.	8 5	1 0	10 5	—
Huntly	9 14	—	11 29	—
Keith Town	9 37	—	12 8p	—
Banff	7 20	—	10 55a	—
Buckie	8 28	—	10 27	—
Elgin	9 30	—	2 40p	—
Ballindalloch, arr.	10 52	2 55	3 40	—

By Motor.	A.M.	P.M.		Passenger Fares from Ballindalloch.
B'dalloch Stn., dep	11 0	3 0	5 45	
Drumin Road	—	—	—	1/-
Downan	—	—	—	1/3
Achbreck	—	—	—	1/6
Tomnavoulin	—	—	—	1/9
Pole Inn	—	—	—	2/-
Tomintoul, arr.	12 40p	4 30	7 25	*3/-

TOMINTOUL TO BALLINDALLOCH.

By Motor.	A.M.	P.M.	Weds. & Sats. P.M.	Passenger Fares from Tomintoul.
Tomintoul, dep.	8 30	2 0	—	6 30	
Pole Inn	—	—	—	—	1/-
Tomnavoulin	—	—	—	—	1/3
Achbreck	—	—	—	—	1/6
Downan	—	—	—	—	1/9
Drumin Road	—	—	—	—	2/-
B'dalloch Stn., ar.	10 0	3 30	—	8 0	*3/-

By Train.	A.M.	P.M.		P.M.	
Ballindalloch, de.	10 13	5 38	—	8 36	—
Elgin	11 25	6 50	—	—	—
Buckie	12 53p	7 57	—	—	—
Banff	12 45	8 50	—	—	—
Keith Town	11 21a	6 52	—	—	—
Huntly	11 53	9 1	—	—	—
Aberdeen, arr.	12 55p	10 10	—	10 32	—

* Return Fare, Ballindalloch and Tomintoul, 5/-

June 1914 timetable for the buses to Tomintoul. The Wednesday and Saturday runs were in connection with the excursions from Aberdeen.

This appears to have been aimed at the tourist traffic, including the popular circular tours via Deeside, Donside and Speyside described on page 60.

The full impact of the timber resources on the railway did not become apparent until the Great War of 1914-18 when the Canadian Forestry Corps set up a number of sawmills on Speyside to exploit them. Virtually all of the timber produced would have gone out by rail but, although there seems to be no surviving record of the amount involved, it was certainly enough to justify the Great North laying down a timber siding near Knockando and two more at Nethy Bridge. Much obviously came in by road but at least one of the two at Nethy Bridge had a narrow gauge railway connecting it with the surrounding woods.

The Knockando siding was lifted in 1920 but was promptly re-laid for use by Messrs Syme of Inverness. During the same year another siding was provided about 600 yards north of Ballindalloch for use by Messrs Black from Brechin who also loaded considerable quantities at Blacksboat.

The 1922 timetable, the last under GNSR ownership, showed that mixed trains had disappeared as had the Ballindalloch locals. Journey times were around 1 hour 10 minutes giving an overall average speed of around 28-29 miles per hour.

The GNSR's ownership of the Strathspey line ended on 31st December 1922. The following day the Great North became the Northern Scottish Area of the newly formed London & North Eastern Railway. Exactly twenty five years later the LNER itself was absorbed by British Railways.

Looking west on Main Street in Tomintoul, in the days before the First World War, this postcard shows a Great North bus on the left. This was SA875, a Milnes-Daimler 28/ 35hp chassis with a GNSR built body, first registered in April 1912.
(Keith Jones collection)

LNER and British Railways Days

The change of management in 1923 did not result in great changes along Speyside; the line was, after all, the furthest outpost of the new company. At Boat of Garten, connection was now made with the London, Midland & Scottish Railway. Road transport offered increasing competition to the railways nationally, but the remoteness of the Spey Valley and the slow improvement to the roads in the area delayed the impact locally. With the depression of the 1930s, traffic did fall away and economies, such as staff reduction, were necessary. The loop at Cromdale had been taken out in 1921 but there was little change to the stations during the 1920s and 1930s.

The LNER maintained much the same pattern of three return journeys but at various times during the 1930s took what could be seen as a retrograde step with the re-introduction of mixed trains. Northbound the 1.02pm from Boat of Garten had goods vehicles attached as far as Knockando while southbound the 10.15am departure from Craigellachie became mixed at Ballindalloch. These workings applied Monday to Friday and ceased with the winter timetable for 1937. The September 1938 timetable still showed three passenger trains; the goods service now consisted of two trains the whole length of the line plus one working, when required, conveying horse boxes from Ballindalloch to Craigellachie. On Saturdays the 1.02 pm worked through to Elgin returning from there at 9.05pm. The Company's final time-table still allowed around 77 minutes for the journey.

With such a sparse service, passengers had to fit their day around the available trains. This applied in particular to school children. One former pupil recalled using the train to get from Carron to Aberlour in the early 1920s, as did others from as far up the line as Advie. They arrived at Aberlour at 9.30am. At 3.05pm the "Train Pupils' Bell" rang and they were off on their way home. Their morning arrival could be delayed if the down goods was late.

As with the grouping of 1923, nationalisation in 1948 brought little noticeable change for the first few years. Management was now from British Railways Scottish Region headquarters in Glasgow. By the early 1950s, the switch to road transport resumed its pre-war speed. Nationally, the financial position of the railways was deteriorating and repeated attempts were made to reverse this trend. Branch line closures became the order of the day and it was inevitable that the Speyside line should

A Boat of Garten train awaits departure from Craigellachie. The station approach road, on the right, dropped down between the Speyside and Elgin platforms. One of the few remains of the station today is the platform edge on the left, but it is now in the car park for the Speyside Way and surrounded by trees.
(GNSRA)

The Northern Belle was an inclusive tour train operated by the LNER during the middle and late 1930s. For £20 each, passengers spent a week touring from London as far as Speyside, sleeping on the train. Various excursions were arranged. Some meals were taken on the train, while others were at railway-owned hotels, where dancing could continue well into the night. Group photographs were organised, such as this one at Grantown-on-Spey. *(GNSRA collection)*

be considered. Passenger traffic on the southern end of the line had always been lighter, so in 1955 a proposal was made to withdraw passenger trains between Ballindalloch and Boat of Garten. When the Scottish Transport Users Consultative Committee considered this it received a deputation of representatives of residents of Grantown and Nethy Bridge and the Scottish Tourist Board who explained the problems with bus services in winter months and the effect closure would have on rural depopulation and tourism. The Committee recommended that withdrawal be postponed in this case pending further investigation into the provision of reasonable alternative transport.

By 1956 only the first departure in each direction called at all stations — Advie, Blacksboat and Cromdale being the losers. An interesting innovation occurred in the late 1950s when it was possible to travel in one of two coaches labelled "Boat of Garten" on the 6.47pm departure from Aberdeen. This journey covering 101¼ miles was the longest that could be made on Great North metals without changing trains and previously had only been possible with the Speyside Excursions. The time of 3½ hours was an hour longer than that taken by the those trains 50 years earlier!

The Speyside passenger trains were diagrammed for a single set of carriages which was based at Boat of Garten. In 1947, this consisted of a composite coach with both first and second class accommodation which was sandwiched between two brake third vehicles each of which had a guard's van and third class passenger compartments. The Saturday Only train at 9.45pm from Craigellachie

Table 223 CRAIGELLACHIE and BOAT OF GARTEN

Miles from Craigellachie	Week Days only		p.m.	p.m.	p.m.	Saturdays only p.m
	1 London (King's C.)	dep	7UZ30	7UZ30	10U30	
	184 Glasgow (Q.St.)	"	..	..	8a41	1250
	184 Edinburgh (Wav	"	4a10	4a10	10 0	2 15
	217 Aberdeen	"	8 5	9 30	3p30	7Y15
—	Craigellachie	dep	10 25	3p0	6p45	9 45
2¼	Aberlour		10 30	3 5	6 50	9 50
—	Dailuaine Halt		Aa	Aa	Aa	Aa
5¾	Carron..............		10 39	3 13	6 58	9 58
8¼	Knockando............		10 44	3 20	7 3	10 3
10½	Blacksboat............		10 49	3 25	7 8	10 8
12¼	Ballindalloch..........		10 56	3 31	7 15	1013
15¼	Advie		11 3	3 38	7 22	1019
21¼	Cromdale............		11 14	3 49	7 33	1029
24	Grantown-on-Spey.......		11 21	3 56	7 40	1035
28¾	Nethy Bridge..........		11 33	4 8	7 52	1044
33½	Boat of Garten.....	arr	11 42	4 17	8 3	1052

Miles	Week Days only		a.m.	p.m.	p.m
—	Boat of Garten.....	dep	8 8	12 52	4 50
4¾	Nethy Bridge...........		8 17	1 2	4 59
9½	Grantown-on-Spey.......		8 26	1 11	5 8
12¼	Cromdale............		8 32	1 17	5 14
18¼	Advie..............		8 43	1 27	5 24
21¼	Ballindalloch..........		8 52	1 34	5 31
23	Blacksboat............		8 57	1 39	5 36
25½	Knockando............		9 3	1 45	5 42
27¾	Carron..............		9 11	1 51	5 48
—	Dailuaine Halt		Aa	Aa	Aa
31½	Aberlour		9 21	2 1	5 59
33½	Craigellachie	arr	9 28	2 7	6 4
101½	217 Aberdeen	arr	12p21	4 47	9 0
231¾	184 Edinburgh (Wav)	"	4 25	9 15	9A38
261¾	184 Glasgow (Q.St.)	"	5 59	10 19	11A4
624¾	1 London (King's C.)	"	5a5	6a30	6F0

A a.m. Except Suns.
a a.m.
Aa Stops when required. Passengers wishing to alight must inform Guard
P p.m. Except Suns.
p p.m.
S Saturdays only
U Applies Weekdays (except Saturdays) and Sundays
Y Dep. 7 25 p.m. until 20th September incl.
Z Limited Sleeping accommodation between King's Cross and Aberdeen.

One of the last LNER timetables, October 1947

consisted of an identical 3 coach set sent from Elgin to Craigellachie by the 6.5am Goods on the Saturday morning and returned to Elgin on Mondays by the 8.30am Goods from Boat of Garten.

During the 1950s, the formation was just two coaches and the Saturday through service from Aberdeen often just a single coach.

So far as the maintenance of connections at Craigellachie was concerned the instructions were unequivocal: "All connections at Craigellachie to and from Speyside stations with main line trains are to be maintained."

Meanwhile, the Modernisation Plan for British Railways had been announced. This aimed to eliminate the financial deficit by investing in diesel traction and the modernising freight handling, including concentration on a smaller number of mechanised freight depots. For rural lines such as Speyside, 4-wheeled railbuses were proposed and these were introduced with some flourish on the Speyside line in 1958. As a precursor, a railbus was sent to Elgin for inspection by various dignitaries on 19th September. The Lord Lieutenant of Moray described it as "a day of history in the county." Local Government and British Railways officials, including the Scottish Region deputy chairman, Cameron of Lochiel, were there, and so was Major the Hon Robert Bruce, representing the Scottish Council (Development and Industry)

Table 41 — AVIEMORE, BOAT OF GARTEN, GRANTOWN, CRAIGELLACHIE and ELGIN

Down direction (Aviemore to Elgin):

Miles	Station
—	Aviemore ... dep
5¼	Boat of Garten ... arr / dep
10	Nethy Bridge Halt
12	Ballifurth Farm Halt
14¼	Grantown-on-Spey (East)
17¾	Cromdale
21	Dalvey Farm Halt
23½	Advie
26¾	Ballindalloch
28¼	Blacksboat
30¼	Knockando
30½	Gilbey's Cottages Halt
32¼	Imperial Cottages Halt
33	Carron
34	Dailuaine Halt
36¼	Aberlour
38¼	Craigellachie ... arr / dep
41¼	Rothes
48¼	Longmorn
51¼	Elgin ... arr

Up direction (Elgin to Aviemore):

Miles	Station
—	Elgin ... dep
3	Longmorn
9¾	Rothes
12¼	Craigellachie ... arr / dep
14¾	Aberlour
17¾	Dailuaine Halt
18¼	Carron
18½	Imperial Cottages Halt
20¼	Gilbey's Cottages Halt
20½	Knockando
23	Blacksboat
24½	Ballindalloch
27¾	Advie
30¼	Dalvey Farm Halt
33¾	Cromdale
36¾	Grantown-on-Spey (East)
39¾	Ballifurth Farm Halt
41¼	Nethy Bridge Halt
46	Boat of Garten ... arr / dep
51¼	Aviemore ... arr

Footnotes:

b   Arr. 2 minutes later on Saturdays
E   Except Saturdays
S   Saturdays only
TC Through Carriages
zz Calls to set down on notice to Guard or to take up when there are passengers on platform
Ⓢ Second class only

The September 1964 passenger timetable – not long before closure

No.62277 'Gordon Highlander' leaves Craigellachie with the 2.55pm to Boat of Garten in June 1956. Apart from the goods shed on the right, the buildings had hardly altered in ninety years. Two coach trains were the usual formation by then.   *(F G Wood/GNSRA collection)*

which had persuaded BR to introduce the railbus to fend off the closure mooted in 1956. Later the railbus went to Aviemore where it was open for public inspection.

With the introduction of the railbus on 3rd November 1958, a real attempt was made to make the service more attractive. Not only was the journey time from Boat of Garten to Craigellachie now reduced to 68 minutes, but four new request stops were opened on 15th June 1959. These just required track-level platforms as the railbuses were equipped with steps; not easy to negotiate if you were infirm but considered acceptable at the time. Furthermore, the service was extended through to Aviemore at the south end, for which a new crossover was installed at Boat of Garten, and two trains were extended to Keith. The late Saturday train with its through coaches from Aberdeen remained locomotive hauled. The depot at Boat of Garten was closed and all remaining crews moved to Aviemore. At that time this was still just a village of about 600 people, many employed by the railway, but at least it did offer better connections than Boat of Garten. Tickets were now issued on the train, not only for the new halts but for all the other stations, although clerks were retained at stations for goods and parcel traffic administration.

Passengers join a Wickham built railbus at Gilbey's Cottages Halt. There was no requirement for disabled access then.

(E Heleas)

In the late 1950s, the railway still carried a considerable non-passenger traffic by passenger train. This could range from parcels to livestock such as day old chicks. Mail order became popular at this time for household items and most were delivered by rail. The livestock sales at Ballindalloch Mart produced traffic. One dealer in Archiestown sold working dogs through the weekly publication *Exchange and Mart* and shipped them from Carron. Although agitated, they were looked after well by the railwaymen, as were pigs in crates, calves in sacks, etc. Little of this traffic could be carried by the railbus so most was transferred to the goods trains. The distilleries received much traffic this way, so were not impressed at the extended transit times

The railbuses quickly acquired the nickname "Sputnik" after the Soviet satellite which was first launched in 1957. They were equipped with a central, power operated door on each side and sat about 50, second class only of course, in bus-type seats arranged to face each end. There was limited storage space in the centre. Drivers cabs were half width, with a rear-facing seat along the front of the vehicle. The windows at the ends offered excellent views of the scenery and gave the vehicles a very modern appearance. Typical vehicle weight was about 13 or 14 tons, about half an ordinary bogie coach. But they were still four-wheelers and not good riders. There was of course no need now for a fireman, so operating costs were reduced.

At the four halts provided for the railbus, a wooden board was provided to remind the drivers. The paint did not last long,

(J L Stevenson)

Moreover, British Railways had ordered small batches of vehicles from several manufacturers. As some were chosen for their knowledge of bus building, the railbuses were not designed for the rigours of railway conditions and they were not very reliable. Perhaps if only one type had been ordered and more effort put into making that work well, the story would have turned out differently. Suffice to say that within 10 years of introduction, the railbuses had passed into history. When a railbus was not available, a locomotive and coach had to be used, steam hauled at first then diesel hauled after 1961. Passengers for the new halts then had to use a ladder, no fun with shopping bags full of purchases.

Changes to the services on the main line through Craigellachie led to alteration of the Speyside service from June 1961. One train now ran through to Elgin rather than Keith and the Saturday through coach from Aberdeen was withdrawn, replaced by giving the railbus an additional evening run. To squeeze this in, the previous down working terminated at Grantown so that the railbus could return to Craigellachie in time to make the connection.

A journey on a Saturday in 1963 illustrated the use made of the line at the time. The railbus was almost empty from Aviemore, not picking up many passengers until Cromdale. The vehicle became more and more crowded at the next few stops as people with empty shopping bags joined, but nearly all got off at Aberlour. A few more joined during the rest of the journey to Elgin, by which time the through passenger from Aviemore felt a bit sea-sick! Curiously the return journey was much quieter; where the people who left at Aberlour on the outward run went was a mystery, unless there was a more convenient bus or they spent several hours at Aberlour.

Great North of Scotland Railway.

LUGGAGE.

GRANTOWN-ON-SPEY

FROM ABERDEEN.

The railbuses used in the last few years were not very reliable so quite often a substitute had to be found. Here D5341 hauls an LMS Brake Third on an Aviemore bound train at Cromdale. One coach was quite sufficient, as it had about the same seating capacity as the railbus. The crew wait patiently while the local postman loads mail. (*David Sleight/GNSRA*)

D8030 making up its train at Craigellachie in preparation for a run down the valley. Quite a mixture of wagons can be seen, including three open ones carrying whisky barrels, a couple of coal hoppers and several vans. The English Electric Type 1 (later Class 20) was one of several types of diesel loco used on the line. (*J L Stevenson*)

Decline and Closure

The Modernisation Plan had failed to stem the losses made by British Railways, so drastic action was taken by the government of the day. Dr Beeching was appointed chairman of the British Transport Commission in 1961 and in 1963 produced his solution, which included the closure of many lines. Not only was the Speyside line included, but all those in the north of Scotland except the direct lines from Inverness to Perth and Aberdeen.

When the closure of the Speyside line was considered by the Transport Users Consultative Committee, BR complained that the introduction of the railbus had failed to encourage local people to use the line. Objections came from the tourist industry as development of Aviemore as a ski resort was just beginning but in practice the Speyside line would have been of little use to skiers who tended to come from Central Scotland and more often by road. Local representatives claimed that the railway was essential for the developing winter sports trade at Grantown-on-Spey, but the Scottish Region claimed that no more than 20 skiers a week on average were taking advantage of cheap winter holiday fare offers. In general, according to the Scottish Region, the railbus had seldom carried more than ten passengers.

It came as little surprise that closure was approved and passenger trains were withdrawn as from Monday 18th October 1965, a week later than originally intended due to insufficient notice of closure having been given. Some additional bus services were provided to compensate. The final passenger trains between Craigellachie and Aviemore ran on 16th October 1965 but on that day the railbus operated only the first return working from Aviemore and was then replaced by English Electric Type 1 (later Class 20) D8028 hauling two coaches to handle the influx of passengers from the south. These locos were not equipped to provide train heating. To allow for those taking souvenir photographs the train departed 3 minutes late but a further 3 minutes were dropped to Aberlour by one of those incidents that can only happen on a rural branch line. Two young stirks had strayed on to the railway and had to be gently edged out of the way by diesel hoots! The conditional stops were called at Dailuaine and Gilbey's Cottages. Passengers on this train had to climb down a short ladder and as three of them had very obviously been celebrating the problems can be imagined. There was the usual delay at Nethy Bridge where the second man on the loco had to open and close the level-crossing gates but even so arrival at Aviemore was one minute early.

D8028 also headed the 4.50pm departure which was delayed five minutes in consequence. The conditional stops at Ballifurth and Dalvey were not called and, with no traffic on offer, both Advie and Blacksboat were passed non-stop, thus allowing the train to be on time by Knockando. The three remaining conditional stops at Gilbey's, Imperial and Dailuaine were all called, the first two once again bringing the ladder into use. Thus the final train ran into Craigellachie one minute late at 6.09pm. The connecting trains, to Elgin and Keith, were already in the station and so for the last time all three platforms at the station were occupied simultaneously.

By 1964 two daily goods trains sufficed from Mondays to Fridays with only one on Saturdays, still generous by the standards of most other lines at that time. By this time wagonload traffic was not considered desirable and since distillery work was mostly of this type, it was discouraged. No distillery could justify a weekly block train of coal or whisky. When a ten-year agreement was signed to transport malting barley by rail from East Anglia to Dufftown, grain silos were erected at Dufftown and it soon became the point for distribution by road to most of the distilleries down Speyside.

Passenger services from Keith to Elgin through Craigellachie were withdrawn in May 1968.

The Speyside line could not be supported by the remaining traffic so it closed south of Aberlour as from Monday 4th November 1968, when the freight trains on the Craigellachie to Elgin section also ceased.

The last goods ran on 1st November when the 10.10am left Aviemore well loaded with 16 wagons of coal. By the time it arrived at Craigellachie several more wagons carrying whisky and general merchandise had been added. From the following Monday the coal would have to take the long way round via Aberdeen while the whisky went by rail via Elgin or road all the way.

The final train was a "Speyside Excursion" which ran on Saturday 2nd November. Organised by the GNSR Association, it was made up of three corridor coaches headed by Type 2 (later Class 26) No.D5313 and set off from Aberdeen Joint Station at 9.30am. With over 130 people on board it stopped specially at Insch to pick up eight more passengers and following a crew change at Keith had the line to itself. Dufftown saw a further four passengers join and after that it was a case of all stations to Aviemore. At each, passengers rushed out, took their photographs and then rushed back on board. As the train progressed up the Spey valley, the snow on the ground grew deeper.

O wae's me for Craigellachie
Whaur Grants stood fast of yore!
Thon station braw will silent be,
The Sodger seen no more
Change here no more for sweet Strathspey
On shining summer morns,
And here no more when cattle stray
Will diesels toot their horns!
Those golden woods by Tunnel Brae,
The river shining clear;
All nature's glorious panoply
Throughout the changing year...
These will remain, yet thou art gone,
Thou pilgrim of the sleepered way!
That we no more may journey on
When the Auld Line's away!
The Auld Line! The Auld Line!
By Carron, Advie and Dalvey!
What can replace youth's rapture fine
When the Auld Line's away!

Cuthbert Graham in the *Press and Journal* for 2nd November 1968, the day of the very last train over the Speyside Line. "The Sodger" was the nick-name of No.62277 *Gordon Highlander*. Reproduced by kind permission of the Editor of the *Press and Journal*.

No doubt it was a coincidence but the train arrived at Aberlour just as the local hostelry, then the Station Hotel but now the Mash Tun, opened for business and quite a few passengers took advantage of this!

Not much traffic today at Grantown-on-Spey as the signalman carries the single line token to the driver of the 12.25pm Park Royal-built railbus from Aviemore to Elgin in June 1962. (Roy Hamilton)

In spite of the wintry conditions the sun did shine at times and highlighted the autumn colours, which helped to brighten up what was, after all, a somewhat sad occasion.

At Aviemore Piper Donald Brough, a member of the station staff, appeared in full Highland dress and, after entertaining the passengers, piped a farewell as the train left. The return journey was a good deal quicker than the outward one, being virtually non-stop. Craigellachie was reached in gathering darkness and to avoid too early an arrival at Keith there was a prolonged stop during which "a good time was had by all" – the Fiddichside Inn did well! Passengers had come from all parts of Britain, a few to traverse the line for the first and last time. Some local inhabitants were also aboard making a sentimental journey. And then there was Peter McLean, an old driver from the Boat, celebrating his 83rd birthday.

Truly the Speyside Line was seen out in style.

At Aberlour itself coal traffic lingered on for another three years until that too ceased from 15th November 1971. So ended 108 years of service, unspectacular though it may have been, to the local community.

The rails south of Aberlour were lifted during 1969 but in due time this had a happy outcome for walkers. On 3rd July 1981 the Speyside Way was opened, an integral part using the trackbed between Craigellachie and Nethy Bridge, although there are sections between Ballindalloch and Cromdale and between Cromdale and Grantown which are not used. These 28¾ miles provide a truly delightful path through trees and fields, alongside the river and passing three of the distilleries which did so much to give life to the old railway. Whether taking a short stroll or a serious long distance walk, there is something for everyone to enjoy.

Passengers on the very last train, the special organised by the GNSRA on 2nd November 1968, make the most of the opportunity to photograph Grantown-on-Spey East.   *(Keith Fenwick)*

An early panorama of Craigellachie. Railwaymen pose patiently for the photographer beside a class 28 of 1862 standing at the Speyside branch platform. Double armed signals in the centre of the station control traffic on the main line. The shed behind the loco was for stabling carriages; the varnish used at that time did not stand well to the effects of weather.   *(GNSRA collection)*

Craigellachie in 1967, seen from the opposite hillside to the view above. Passenger trains still run on the main line and the sidings are well used. The turntable and adjacent tracks have been removed.   *(Norris Forrest)*

Along The Line

Much of the route now forms part of the Speyside Way which first opened in 1981 from Spey Bay to Ballindalloch using the trackbed of the Speyside Railway from Craigellachie. A spur to Tomintoul was added in 1990 and the route was further extended from Ballindalloch to Aviemore in April 2000. At one time it was hoped that most of this would be on the trackbed, but it was only possible to use a short section south from Ballindalloch and another of about a mile past Cromdale station. The full route is only suitable for walkers, but cyclists and horse riders can use the section from Craigellachie to Ballindalloch.

As well as describing what was to be seen when the railway was operational, remains of the railway which can be seen today are described in this chapter. The

OS Maps

These have been reproduced, by permission of the Trustees of the National Library of Scotland, from the 6 inch to one mile 2nd edition (1902-1909), reduced by 50%. The broken line which runs along the River Spey on some maps marks the county border between Morayshire and Banffshire.

Abbreviations:
C   Crane
FB   Footbridge
FP   Footpath
GP   Guide Post
MP   Mile Post
P   Pump
PH   Public House
PO   Post Office
SB   Signal Box
SP   Signal Post
WM   Weighing Machine

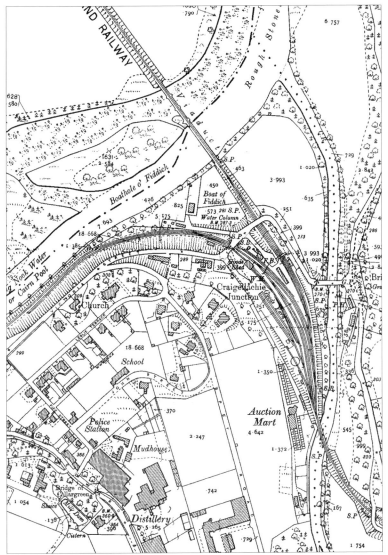

Craigellachie was closely confined by the rivers Fiddich and Spey. The main line from Aberdeen to Elgin is on the right with the Speyside line curving away to the left towards Aberlour.

Craigellachie from the south, with the platforms for the main line to Elgin on the right and the Speyside platform on the left. The main signal box was at the south end of the loop; the one visible controlled the points at the far end of the branch platform.   *(G N Turnbull/GNSRA)*

terms 'north' and south' are used to refer to the Craigellachie and Boat of Garten ends of the line respectively, although it generally follows a north east to south west course. The 'Down' direction was to Boat of Garten and 'Up' to Aberdeen, but this was reversed between Boat of Garten and Aviemore, where 'Up' was towards Perth. OS National Grid References are given for the stations together with distance from Craigellachie.

Legally the Strathspey Railway began at Dufftown but, when completed, the first four miles, which dropped steeply down Glen Fiddich to Craigellachie, became part of the main Aberdeen-Elgin route and so do not form part of the Speyside line story.

Craigellachie station (NJ 264 429) lay in the angle between the Elgin and Strathspey lines with the latter on the west side of the layout. The layout was confined by the rivers Fiddich and Spey. There were two platforms on the Elgin line and one on the branch. The yard on the west side of the line included a goods shed, loading docks and turntable. The extensive sidings were used to keep a supply of wagons for Speyside; if a station needed wagons to transport whisky, a request was sent to Craigellachie for them. Originally there had been a carriage shed on the site of the later goods shed. As well as the main signal box at the south end of the station, there was a smaller one on the

The western portal of the tunnel at Craigellachie, showing the steep hillside into which the railway had to be built.
(G N Turnbull/GNSRA)

The difficulty of constructing this section of the line is illustrated in this photograph of the last up goods train in 1968 between Aberlour and Craigellachie. *(Aberdeen Journals)*

branch platform. Nowadays it is hard to visualise the comparative complexity of the junction. The A95 from Keith used to cross the lines on two separate bridges, where it is now on an embankment. All the buildings have been demolished. The Elgin platforms have gone but part of the Speyside platform remains, covered in trees in what is now a picnic area and car park. The base of the signal box forms a viewing platform looking out over the River Fiddich and the site of the turntable can still be distinguished.

On leaving Craigellachie, the railway curved sharply to the south-west to follow the right bank of the River Spey. Just past this point, looking right offers views across to the imposing Manor House at Easter Elchies, now the home of The Macallan Distillery, and to the famous single arch span Craigellachie Bridge built by engineer Thomas Telford in 1814. The Craigellachie bypass now intersects the trackbed but an underpass has been built for users of the Speyside Way. The line then ran through a short tunnel, which had portals but was unlined and was one of only four on the whole Great North system, before again reaching the Spey where it ran on a ledge cut out of the steep bank above the water. A massive retaining wall about 40 feet high and 100 yards long was needed here.

Aberlour (2¾ miles, NJ 265 429) lies in wider area of the valley with the river now further away from the station. The town, which was the only place of any size served directly by the line, developed along the main road northwards from the station. The local distillery was a useful source of traffic. The station was also the commercial hub of the line as the station was in easy walking distance of a bank. Cash collected at each station was sent by train and "paid in" at Aberlour. The station building remains here and is now owned by Moray Council. It still has the drinking fountain body and a Great North lamp arm unusually affixed on the corner of the

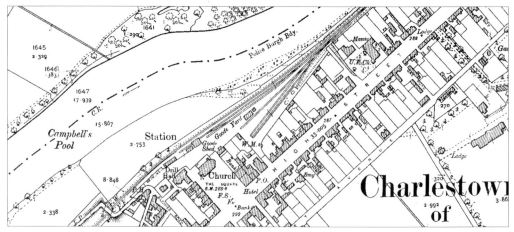

At Aberlour the passing loop was not added until 1910, several years after this map was surveyed.

building at an angle. The building cost £219 in 1863, about the same as the other original station buildings at Carron, Blacksboat, Ballindalloch, Cromdale, Grantown and Nethy Bridge. However, it has features not found on these other buildings, such as the gables on the platform side and in particular the central decorated one, and the rear extension, so it may have been rebuilt. Photos show it in its present form in the early 1900s, including the surface rendering which is not found elsewhere on the line. In 2004 the building was extended at the south end using modern materials but in architectural sympathy with the original style to accommodate an interesting Visitor Display Centre for the Speyside Way and its Ranger Service and although this extends into the original building, there remains space for a tea room.

The yard and goods shed were at the north end and continued in use by the local coal merchant until the 1990s. In recent years this has given way to a modern housing development known as

Aberlour was rebuilt in 1910 with a passing loop and new up platform, seen on the left. No.70, a class G (D48), heads a Boat of Garten train sometime prior to 1923.   *(J R Kerby collection)*

The last Speyside train ran in November 1968 at Aberlour. The goods yard continued in use for coal traffic and was still busy.   *(Keith Fenwick)*

"Station Court". The second platform, which was added after the accompanying map was surveyed, has been removed completely and the area between the station and the river laid out as the Alice Littler Memorial Park. The Aberlour Highland Games are held here on the first Saturday in August. The line passed under the bridge at the south end of the station which now leads to the car park.

The line continues along the east bank of the Spey and before long the hillside crowds in again and at 4¼ miles, cut into the steep bank, is the small platform of **Dailuaine** (NJ 237 413), opened in 1933 for the benefit of the workers at this isolated distillery; it has been restored and with a picnic table and litter bin added now boasts more facilities than during the time the railway operated. Three quarters of a mile further on came the distillery's private siding which trailed in on the left but it is hard to see any remains at this locations. It passed under the adjacent road at an angle. However, if you travel back along the road to Dailuaine Distillery the locomotive shed and road

Aberlour looking south in 1968 when only goods trains operated. Compare this with the current scene on page 54; the up platform has disappeared and the area is now grassed over. An extension has been added to the station building to house the Visitor Centre for the Strathspey Way. (G N Turnbull/ GNSRA)

The LNER halt at Dailuaine was a simple platform accessed from a path which conveniently crossed the line at that point.
(GNSRA collection

The exchange siding at Dailuaine, seen from the road which crossed it at an angle. The left-hand track continued to the distillery. The distillery pug is sandwiched between a covered wagon and an open one loaded with whisky barrels. (GNSRA collection)

A Craigellachie-bound train crossing Carron viaduct on 22nd July 1958. The roadway was on the downstream side of the bridge. The locomotive, a Fowler LMS 2-2T No.40011, was a stranger to the area but worked the line for some weeks.
(Charles Dick)

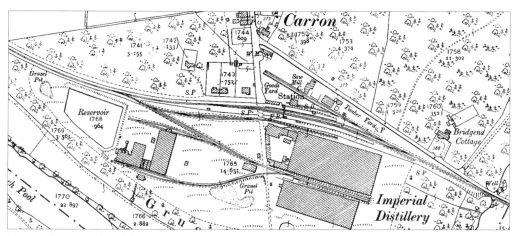

The small community of Carron was dominated by Imperial Distillery, which was squeezed in between the railway and the river. The owner of the sawmill chose a handy site alongside both road and railway

over-bridge are still intact and the line of the track is still discernible.

Returning to the Speyside line, shortly afterwards it crossed the Spey on a fine cast-iron arch bridge built by Mackinnon & Co, Engineers, Aberdeen, with a span of some 150 feet which it shared with what is now a public road. Originally this provision was made for the benefit of Mr Grant of Carron but there is no evidence that he paid the extra cost of £1,500 involved! For many years, no attempt was made to use the trackbed to widen the road but in 2010 a footpath was constructed on it. You have to go down to the river's edge to get a proper appreciation of the bridge.

Carron (5½ miles, NJ 221 412) is on the far side of the bridge and had a passing place and small goods yard on the west side of the line. The station building can have altered little from the day it

Carron station, looking south, in GNSR days with an interesting group of people which includes railwaymen, children and possibly the local tramp. The wooden footbridge and goods shed on the right were typical Great North designs.
(Mike Stephen/GNSRA)

Carron on 7th June 1958 looking towards Craigellachie. Everything is in good order. The goods shed is now painted in cream or off-white. The post at the end of the platform on the right was for the automatic tablet exchanger, a facility which was mainly used on the Speyside line for some of the goods trains and the summer excursions. *(GNSRA collection)*

was built, when it cost £214, except that the centre frontage on the platform side was enclosed by a wooden and glass partition in the late nineteenth century. This happened at all the stations along the line. Like every station with a passing place, the opposite platform just had a small wooden shelter, partly open at the front. There was a goods yard, complete with shed, behind the station building and a signal box on the Up platform.

Again the hills are very close although the level ground between the station and the river was occupied by the Imperial Distillery, one of the largest in the area, and its extensive bonded warehouses. These were served by sidings south of the station. Since closure of the line, the station site was purchased by Imperial Distillery and landscaped. The distillery was mothballed by Allied Distillers in 1998 and, though sold to Pernod Ricard in 2005, remains silent.

The next five miles to Blacksboat brought their own problems when the railway was built. The ground rises steeply from the river, which itself follows a very sinuous course, leading to some heavy earthworks. In addition, there are a number of burns to cross, often in quite deep gullies. One of these, formed by the Allt Adhair, called for a substantial three span viaduct some 50 feet above the ground; all the more

Imperial Cottages was one of the four 'bus-stop' halts erected by British Railways to take advantage of the folding steps on the railbuses. (Keith Fenwick)

Knockando House Platform, seen in 1960, consisted of a simple wooden platform - no name, no lights. Access was via a footpath at the far end.

(Norris Forrest/GNSRA)

remarkable since the burn is almost narrow enough to jump across.

This stretch had several interesting features including two created by British Railways as 'bus-stop' halts to serve isolated distillery communities. They did not even have platforms since they were served by the diesel rail buses which had retractable steps. **Imperial Cottages Halt** (6 miles, NJ 215 415) is marked by a gate in the fence and a length of upright rail with a damaged LNER trespass sign. Next came the only stop on this part of the line which dates from its early days. **Knockando House** (7 miles, NJ 205 423) was a private platform strictly reserved, at least originally, for the owner of the house and his factor and "only during the pleasure of the Directors." It was known as plain Knockando until 1905, when Dalbeallie was renamed Knockando. Even in BR days it remained unadvertised but it was included in the stops made by the last train down the line in 1968. Around here, some bridges were demolished after the line closed and had to be replaced to create the Speyside Way. For instance, just north of Knockando House, a wooden bridge on the original stone pillars carries the Way over Ballintomb Burn.

The other BR halt, **Gilbey's Cottages** (8 miles, NJ 193 415) actually served Knockando Distillery, 7¼ miles, which had a siding; the loading bank and crane can still be seen in the distillery grounds. Not long before it was completed the owners decided that they wanted the loading bank higher than was originally agreed so as to make it easier to move barrels out of the adjoining warehouse.

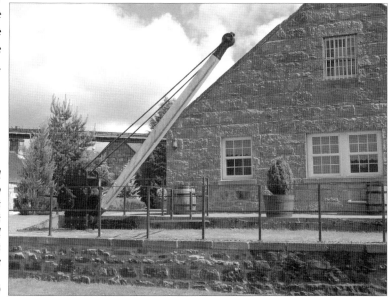

The loading bank and crane at Knockando Distillery have been kept as reminders of the past in the well-maintained premises which can easily be seen from the Strathspey Way.

(Keith Fenwick)

Gilbey's Cottages halt was one of those designed for use by the railbuses. When loco haulage had to be substituted, passengers had to use the emergency ladder in the guard's van. They had more difficulty getting on and off, but there were similar steps to negotiate at the boundary fence.
(Graham Maxtone collection)

This brought a curt response from the GNSR's engineer who pointed out that this would create considerable difficulties in loading casks: it would be impossible to lower the doors of open wagons and van doors would also be blocked. The original height was quickly agreed to! The Halt was at the other end of the distillery.

A few years after the line opened, the residents around Knockando petitioned for a platform to allow them to use the trains. This was turned down by the directors who told them the remedy was "a new road to Carron station." It is clear from the correspondence about Knockando House platform that the laird of Carron was not in favour of this idea!

When in 1896 Tamdhu Distillery was opened on another piece of level ground beside the railway, it was provided with a private siding but on 1st July 1899 a proper station was opened. Known first as **Dalbeallie** (pronounced Dal-bee-alley) it finally became **Knockando** (8¼ miles, NJ 191 416) in 1905. In case passengers were confused by the lack of a footbridge between platforms, they were reminded by a sign to "Cross The Line By The Subway Only" – an arrangement seen only at one other place on the Great North.

After closure, the station building was adapted as a visitor centre for Tamdhu distillery, but this facility has since closed. The building and signal box, complete with Stevens lever frame, remain as reminders of the attractive design of Great North of Scotland stations in the late nineteenth century when most were constructed in wood but with much more ornamentation than is found on the

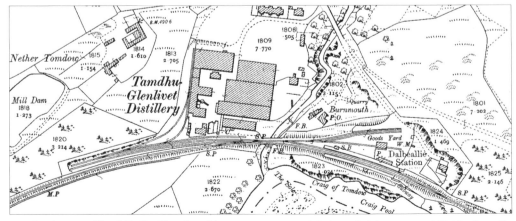

Knockando was still call Dalbeallie when this map was surveyed. It is tucked into a steep hillside above the river. The subway, as opposed to a footbridge, is clearly marked.

A nicely posed picture, issued as a postcard, of Knockando before it was renamed in 1905. The sender of the postcard wrote "This is where you used to spend your holidays" on it. (Ross Kerby/GNSRA)

Knockando station in 1989 when it was in use as the visitor centre for Tamdhu Distillery. At that time, one of its functions was to offer samples to visitors. The building was a typical GNSR design of the 1890s, in contrast to the small stone structures at all the others except Advie.

(Keith Fenwick)

No.62277 'Gordon Highlander' calls at Knockando with a Craigellachie bound train in 1953. The buildings do not appear to have had a lick of paint for many years but the station is well-kept and tidy.
(Graham Maxtone collection)

A freight, likely the 2pm from Boat of Garten, leaving Knockando in the 1950s. The locomotive is an ex-Caledonian Railway 0-6-0, a type common on the freight workings at that time. A down freight, the 12.40pm from Keith, is in the station and Tamdhu distillery is in the background.   (John J Smith/Bluebell Railway)

early stone buildings. Today there are steps down to the river at the north end of the station, often used by canoeists.

Of related railway interest in this area, Scottish Malt Distillers owned a peat moss on the hillside high above Knockando in the direction of Dallas. This was usually worked in the 'silent season' at the distilleries but such was the demand for peat for the distilling process that a monorail was constructed to convey the cut peat across its boggy surface.

The entrance to Knockando in 1989 when still in use as a visitor centre for Tamdhu Distillery. Apart from the modern door on the left side the building still appeared as an passenger would have seen it. (Keith Fenwick)

Blacksboat in the 1950s from the road bridge. The wagons in the siding were quite likely stored there rather than being used for local traffic.
(J L Stevenson)

Nearly every station on the Great North had a goods shed, but now Blacksboat is one of the few remaining. It was refurbished in 2008 and, as a listed building, its future should be secure. (Keith Fenwick)

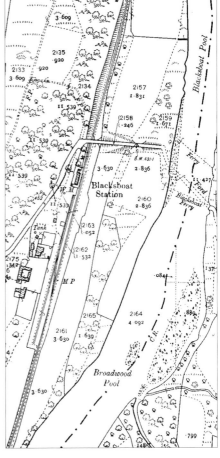

The hills now gradually become less steep and move back from the river so that **Blacksboat** (10½ miles, NJ 183 389) is the last station set into them. For many years the river at this point could only be crossed by ferry despite offers by the railway company to subscribe towards a bridge if others would do likewise. It was not until 1911 that one was finally built. The station building was sold by the Local Authority in 2005 and is now in private use; the goods shed remains at this simple station and both are Category B listed.

About 2 miles further on, the Spey was crossed again, this time by a lattice girder bridge with a span of 198 feet. The contract was almost awarded to the well known firm of Robert Stephenson & Sons who submitted the second lowest tender and were recommended by the Company's engineer on the grounds that nothing

When Blacksboat was surveyed the ferry was still working. An extra siding was added on the west (left) side when the bridge was opened in 1911. The map also shows a ford and a second ferry.

The bridge at Ballindalloch. Since this was taken, in 1989, more trees have grown up to hide it. Inset is the plate on the end of the bridge.   (Keith Fenwick/inset John Ross)

was known of the ability of a Mr McFarlane who made the lowest bid. This was later clarified and as a result this imposing structure still carries plaques on the ends of the girders showing McFarlane as builder. The bridge is now Category A Listed.

Ballindalloch (12¼ miles, NJ 166 366) formed the natural outlet for traffic originating in Glenlivet and, as soon as the railway opened, the Company agreed to donate £50 towards the cost of a coach to be run by George Smith between the station and Tomintoul, 12 miles away, provided it ran daily for two years. Business at the station increased further with the opening of Cragganmore Distillery a short distance away in 1869. Thirty years later the Company bought a small building beside the station which it let to a caterer as a "temperance establishment." This was

A panorama of Ballindalloch from the south, with a railbus about to cross the Spey on its way to Craigellachie. The station retained lower quadrant semaphore signals to the end.   (Real Photographs)

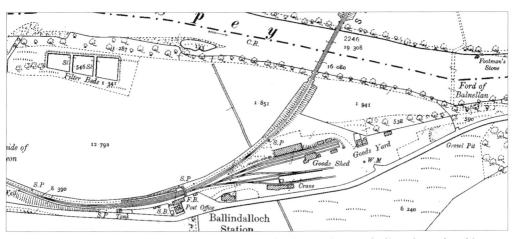

The size of the goods yard at Ballindalloch, compared with other stations on the line, shows that this was a busy place. The filter beds are for yet another distillery, Cragganmore, just off the left hand side of the map.

burnt down in 1905 and promptly re-built. Strangely enough the station itself was virtually gutted by fire in the early hours of 30th May 1922. There was also a cattle mart opposite the station, with a circular wooden building which housed the auction ring, where houses have recently been built. The goods yard, now also occupied by housing, ran parallel to the approach road at the north end of the station; between it and the river was a fine granary which has been converted for residential use. The station building remains, gradually being surrounded by trees, and was used for several years as a hostel. During the time of the railway Ballindalloch had the reputation amongst staff as the equivalent of the Russian Gulag system to which recalcitrants were dispatched to reflect on the error of their ways.

Almost three years after passenger trains ceased, Ballindalloch in June 1968 still retained the air of working station, although it would be closed within six months. As with all stations along the line, the original wooden Great North footbridges were replaced by the LNER using old rails as the main components.

(G N Turnbull/GNSRA)

A northbound train drifts into Ballindalloch in the 1950s, hauled by No.62267, one of the second batch of Class V (D40), built in 1909.   *(G C Bett/GNSRA)*

The Speyside Way takes its own course about a mile south of Ballindalloch while the railway track continues down a now wider valley and then open country to **Advie,** a small station with an interesting history. The original station was about 14½ miles south of Craigellachie but once again there was no bridge over the Spey. One was built in 1869, to which the Company made a contribution of £150, but it was about a half mile south of the station so when it was opened the latter was relocated close to it, at 15¼ miles (NJ 127 346). Originally there was only a mean little wooden station building at Advie, but perhaps the directors felt that Lady Seafield, who lived nearby at Tulchan Lodge, deserved better especially as she entertained royalty; the Prince of Wales, later Edward VII, was a regular visitor. So the building was replaced in 1896 by a rather more lavish wooden structure. As one of the lesser used stations on the line, staff were withdrawn and the small goods yard closed in 1959. The station building soon fell into disrepair and was demolished in the 1970s.

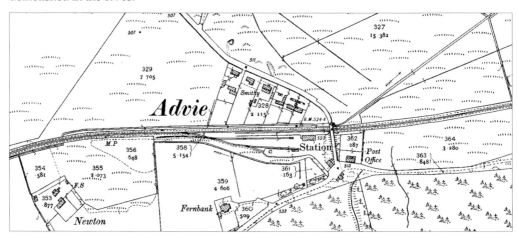

Advie was a small wayside station. Part of the trackbed is now used as the road to the local cemetery.

The lavish wooden building of 1896 at Advie. This is the approach from the road, with the platform on the far side.   *(GNSRA collection)*

The next station, **Dalvey**, 17¼ miles, was only open for a few years as it closed when Advie was moved in 1869. A slight widening of the formation was the only clue to its location. However, the name reappeared nearby when the 'bus-stop' halt was opened Mains of Dalvey farm (NJ 108 321) for the benefit of the local farming community. The halt was just on the Grantown side of the bridge over the river where today there are traffic lights on the A95.

Once more the hills close in and the railway is often close to the river. The Speyside Way rejoins the trackbed just before **Cromdale** (21¼ miles, NJ 071 286) where the country is more open. This small station was the railhead for Balmenach Distillery whose private line, some 1½ miles long, was built in 1897. Again there was no bridge over the Spey until a foot suspension one was opened in 1881, the railway's contribution being the carriage of materials and provision of passes for the workmen. Around 40 years later the Company declined to contribute towards the cost of the road bridge. A passing place was added here in 1907 but was not really needed so it was dispensed with in 1921. The station is now in private ownership, converted into a cosy cottage with an external appearance close to the GNSR style. Many of the fittings have been recreated from original drawings, and behind

For most of its life, Cromdale was a simple wayside station. However, this postcard view, franked 1907, shows the passing loop installed in that year. It was removed in 1921. The footbridge cost £89 in 1907. (A A Keen collection)

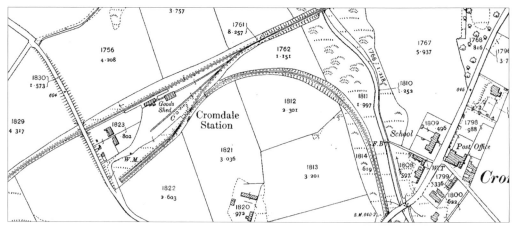

Cromdale, showing the line to Balmenach curving away from the goods yard.

the platform is a wooden carriage body built at Inverurie works in 1916 which is being restored externally to the original style. Although the station yard is now a small settlement of modern houses, it is still possible to trace the route of the distillery branch. Balmenach distillery reopened a few years ago and is owned by the Inver House Distillers Group. There are also two other Great North built houses next to the road. Attached to the south end of the smaller one is the former Up

platform shelter. The Speyside Way finally leaves the trackbed at the road overbridge.

Cromdale looked forlorn in 1969, but the building was still sound and the goods shed extant.
(Keith Fenwick)

Cromdale in 2008, after the station had been converted into residential use and several houses had been constructed on the goods yard. The Speyside Way runs along the trackbed by the platform. The garden on the right is part of the station master's house.
(Keith Fenwick)

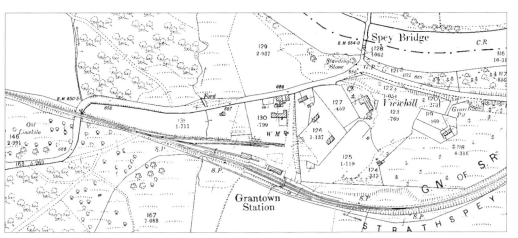

The proximity of the Spey Bridge to the station at Grantown led to it being referred to as Grantown Bridge when the line was inspected prior to opening. The road layout has changed considerably in recent years with the construction of the new Spey Bridge and the road which cuts across the trackbed to the south of the station.

Soon the track was again close to the water before reaching **Grantown** (24¼ miles, NJ 038 261) much the largest town in Strathspey. Geography meant that the Great North station had to be on the opposite side of the river and about a mile from the town, a poorer situation than the rival Highland Railway one. However, the Highland line climbed out of the valley heading over the bleak Dava Moor for Forres while a good deal more business was done by the townsfolk with the various communities in the Strath served by the Speyside line.

For almost the entire history of the line, railway users had to endure the confusion of the rival stations both being called Grantown. Renaming one as Grantown-on-Spey would have helped, but when this happened in 1912, both the Highland and the Great North adopted the longer name! British Railways finally solved the problem by calling the former GNS station Grantown-on-Spey East and re-naming the ex-Highland one Grantown-on-Spey West. Not long after trains began running the Company looked into the possibility of building a hotel beside the station but nothing came of the idea. The station building here was larger than at other stations, but to the same basic design. It was used for storage for many years after closure but is now derelict and is gradually being hidden by the trees which have grown up around it. The realigned A95 cuts across the trackbed at the south end of the station, replacing a road overbridge to the north.

Grantown, looking north, in the 1930s. The original wooden footbridge has yet to be replaced. The shelter on the down platform, another typical GNS design, had disappeared by the 1950s.

(Stations UK)

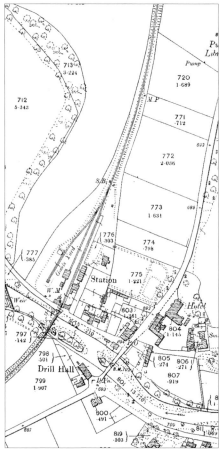

From here on the country is open and, on the south side of the river at least, reasonably flat. The fourth BR 'bus-stop' was near **Ballifurth Farm** (26¾ miles, NJ 014 236) and before long the line reached **Nethy Bridge** (28¼ miles, NJ 000 207) the highest station on the Great North at 690 feet above sea level. Originally called Abernethy it was the terminus of the line until August 1866 and so was complete with engine shed and turntable. It also boasted the line's only public level crossing and this must have caused problems locally as a petition was sent to the directors in 1880. As a result, Mrs McIntyre, the wife of one of the permanent way staff, was appointed as crossing keeper at the wage of 1/- per week plus a house. Twenty five years later she was still there but her pay had risen to 3/6 per week. The station building remains and is now in use as a hostel available to groups. Just beyond the level crossing, the line crossed the Duack Burn.

The railway now turned through almost 90 degrees to run north-west and cross the Spey for the last time by a wooden bridge of six spans. This had been made strong enough to resist the impact of timber being floated down the river and certainly proved its strength in the great Spey flood of February 1868 when it suffered only minor damage despite almost a quarter of a mile of the embankment on the north side being destroyed. Train services were not restored until 1st May. Eighteen months later in December 1869 there was another brief stoppage when ice floes, said to be up to 10 inches thick, damaged one of the piers. Twenty years later it was replaced by a five span steel

Nethy Bridge was the original end of the line, hence the amount of vacant space to the east of the platform. This was occupied by the usual terminal facilities, including turntable and locomotive shed.

Nethy Bridge was a simple station with no passing place. There had been a goods shed on the left. The level crossing was behind the photographer.

(Stations UK)

girder bridge. The piers still stand.

At Tullochgorum, a short distance further on, the line again turned sharply to resume its generally south-west direction and run alongside the Highland's main line from Aviemore to Forres. It was the existence of two separate tracks from here to Boat of Garten which could lead to a race between southbound Great North and Highland trains, but only if the former was running late (or could the Highland be early by any chance?)! Northbound the timetable provided no such opportunities.

By now the country is open and rolling with the Cairngorms in the background - a marked contrast to much of that traversed by the train from Craigellachie. The terminus of the Speyside line at **Boat of Garten**, 33½ miles,

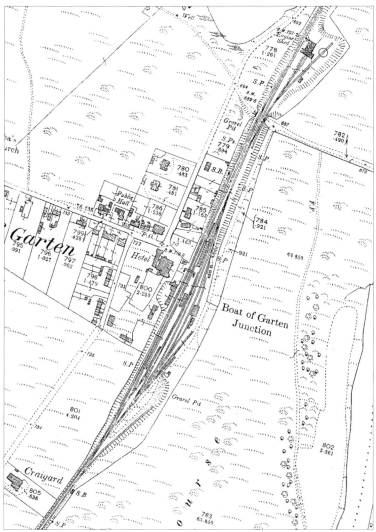

To the north of the station at Boat of Garten, the double track consisted of the Highland main line on the left and the Great North on the right. The extensive layout allowed for exchange of traffic between the two companies.

was a Highland station and all duties were carried out by their employees. For the better part of ninety years Speyside trains had to use the east side of the station, across a footbridge from the main buildings which were on the Down platform. Trains from Speyside could run through the main Up platform and continue on to Aviemore, but through trains coming from Aviemore had an inconvenient shunting manoeuvre to perform. To enable the diesel service to be extended to Aviemore, British Railways installed a cross-over in 1958 which eliminated this awkward arrangement. Because the Speyside service followed the GNSR's normal practice and was based on the country terminus, the Company had its own engine and carriage sheds with supporting staff. The engine shed was tucked out of the way at the north end of the station on a site now mainly occupied by a house.

Those who knew the Strathspey line when it was a working railway will have their memories. The rest can use their imagination : "Did I hear a train?"

A down goods arriving at Boat of Garten behind a D41 No.62231, one of the slightly older GNSR classes, on 4th July 1951. The train is signalled to the Highland up main platform, rather than the bay used by Speyside trains. The Great North loco shed is in the background with one engine being readied to work a northbound train.   *(W A Camwell, courtesy Stephenson Locomotive Society)*

A Great North train is standing at the Speyside platform shortly before leaving for Craigellachie. The Company's carriage shed can be seen beyond the footbridge with the engine shed in the distance.

GNSRA collection)

LNER Class K2 No.61783 'Loch Sheil' at Craigellaichie in April 1956 with a goods train from Aviemore. The correct spelling of the locomotive's name was 'Shiel', but it was never altered. (John McCann/Colour-Rail)

The fine viaduct across the Spey at Ballindalloch has just been crossed by a train bound for Boat of Garten, hauled by an ex-Caledonian 0-6-0. The leading coach is an ex-Great North non-corridor third.

(Colour-Rail.com)

An afternoon train from Boat of Garten calls at Aberlour in the 1950s hauled by 'Gordon Highlander'. The up starter, beyond the footbridge, was on the 'wrong' side of the track because of the curve through the platform.   *(Colour-Rail.com)*

A northbound Park Royal railbus calls at Aberlour one summer afternoon. Mail is waiting to be loaded for its journey to Aberdeen.   *(Chris Gammell)*

You can almost feel the cold in this photograph taken in February 1963 at Grantown-on-Spey. This was one of the coldest winters in memory. The railbus has been replaced by a type 2 diesel and a single coach, with hopefully the steam heating in full operation. With many roads closed, the railways once again came into their own that winter. (Norris Forest)

Undoubtedly the longest train to operate over the Speyside line was the Grand Scottish Tour in March 1967 from Edinburgh back to Edinburgh via Carlisle, Aberdeen, Craigellachie and Aviemore. The curve just south of Nethy Bridge provided an ideal place to capture the length of the train – the photographer was in the third coach. The train included two restaurant cars and required clearance from the Ministry of Transport to operate because of its length. (G N Turnbull/GNSRA)

Advie looking north in 1962. The goods yard, which was on the right, closed in 1959 when the staff were withdrawn. The station building was the one provided as an improvement in 1896 and had more ornamentation than its contemporary Knockando.   *Bob Florence/GNSRA*

Blacksboat is an isolated station but has a wonderful location by the river. Originally there was a ferry here, but a bridge was built in 1911. In recent years, this has been replaced by the concrete structure just visible on the right. When this photograph was taken in 2008, the goods shed had recently been repaired and repainted and the station building adapted as a holiday cottage.   *(Keith Fenwick)*

When the new bridge was built over the Spey at Grantown-on-Spey, the road layout was altered to cut across the track to the south of the station. This is the view from the new road at the north end of the station in June 1992. The station site had been used for a number of years for the storage of pallets, but had been cleared by then and this allowed the trees which today cover the site to grow. (*Keith Fenwick*)

The building at Nethybridge was similar to others along the line, but slightly longer. The wooden front screen was a late Victorian addition. By 1988 when this photograph was taken, its BR brown and cream had been replaced by blue and white. The building continues in use today as a hostel. (*Keith Fenwick*)

Aberlour (above) in June 2008, showing the extension on the right hand end for the Speyside Way visitor centre. The Norman tower of Aberlour Parish Church dates from 1840 while the rest of the church was rebuilt after a disastrous fire in 1861.

(Keith Fenwick)

Other surviving buildings on the section used for the Speyside Way are also well maintained, as at Ballindalloch. The frontage is as rebuilt after the fire of 1922.

(John Ross)

At Dailuaine, the original wooden platform remains, as does the namebaord but it is now mounted on new posts. A pic nic seat provides a useful facility for walkers.

(John Ross)

'Balmenach' approaches the bridge under the A95 on its way from Cromdale to the distillery on 30th June 1965. The Speyside line runs across the field to the left of the engine. *(Peter Tatlow)*

The Balmenach pug shunting at the distillery. The track in the foreground was the end of the branch from Cromdale, with the bonded warehouse and loading point shown on page 68 to the left of the photographer. The line ended to the right of the photographer, so that the loco could shunt into the sidings shown here.

(Graham Maxtone collection)

'Dailuaine' shunting the sidings at the distillery, which is round the corner on the right. The building just visible is the engine shed. (Graham Maxtone collection)

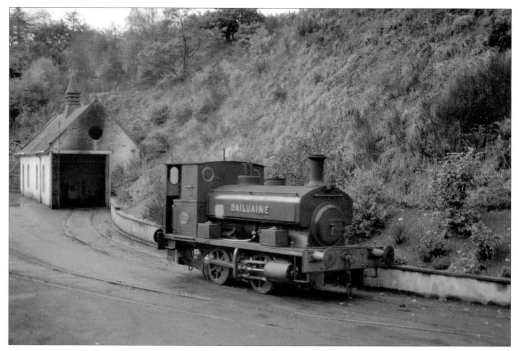

The pug at Dailuaine sits outside its shed in October 1964. The distillery is to the left and the track leading to the Speyside line to the right. The engine shed still survives, as does the locomotive which is now on display at Aberfeldy Distillery. (Mike Stephen/GNSRA)

Locomotives

The Strathspey Railway was the catalyst which led to the Great North being among the first of the British railways to use what became one of the most numerous types of locomotive in the country, the 4-4-0 bogie tender engine. Until the early 1860s, apart from a few small tank engines, the traffic had been worked by 2-4-0 engines and with the impending need to work the Morayshire as well as the Strathspey Railway there was clearly a call for extra engine power. The firm of Robert Stephenson had delivered six 2-4-0s, Class 19, in 1859-61 and it was proposed to order a further nine of the same type. However it seems that Mr Cowan, the Locomotive Superintendent, had doubts about their suitability for the somewhat sinuous line now being considered. The upshot was the decision to build the new engines as 4-4-0s. These became Class 28 and from then on all the Company's tender engines were of this layout.

Shortly after 6pm on 13th September 1878 the peace of Nethy Bridge was shattered when the boiler on one of this class, No.31, exploded. At the subsequent enquiry it was shown that not only was the boiler of poor design but more than 7½ years had elapsed since it was last examined. Although the front part of the boiler was blown some 200 yards from the engine none of the passengers were hurt and of the four men on the footplate only one — an engine cleaner taking an illicit ride — was injured by a piece of flying metal which kept him off work for three weeks.

In subsequent years, the Great North developed the 4-4-0 design, with larger boilers and inside cylinders, culminating in the Class F of 1919/20. One of these, *Gordon Highlander*, has been preserved and is currently at the Scottish Railway Museum in Bo'ness. Generally, as with other branch lines, it was the older engines which worked the Speyside line.

During the 1920s the LNER found that the Great North engines were becoming outclassed due to increasing train weights, and more powerful ones were needed. To begin with these changes did

A new type of engine with a leading bogie was designed for working on the Speyside line. Originally designated Class 28 after the first in the series, they later became Class H. No.35 shown here was built in 1864 and ran without a cab until given a new boiler in 1882. It was withdrawn in 1920. The four wheeled tender allowed the engine to be turned on short turntables. (GNSRA collection)

not affect Speyside, largely because of weight restrictions on the line, but sometime during the war these were relaxed and by 1951 there was at least occasional use of the Class B12 4-6-0s that had come north from the former Great Eastern Railway.

Following Nationalisation in 1948 little changed at first with ex-Great North engines of their Classes F and V, which the LNER had combined into Class D40, virtually monopolising the branch for some years. It was in fact the scene of the last regular working of No.62277 *Gordon Highlander* which outlived all the others and remained in traffic until withdrawn in June 1958 for preservation. Even that was not the end of its active life as it was seen back on Speyside in GNSR livery with a passenger train deputising for a failed railbus as late as 23rd May 1960!

Because the engines were provided by Keith shed other strangers among its allocation put in appearances. At various times in the mid-1950s, ex-LNER Class K2 moguls were used on both goods and passenger trains. Ex-Caledonian Railway 0-6-0s and BR Standard Class 2 2-6-0s were used, with at least one appearance of a pair of the standard Class 4 of the same wheel arrangement on an excursion from Aberdeen. Others noted from time to time included, ex-LNER J36s, LMSR Class 2P 4-4-0s and one example of the same Company's Fowler designed Class 3 2-6-2T, although that engine did not last long in the north east before being sent back south.

In November 1958 steam hauled passenger trains were replaced by 4-wheeled railbuses from three different makers, Bristol, Park Royal and Wickham. All gave an uncomfortable ride and became very unreliable resulting in fairly frequent replacement by a single locomotive hauled coach, as indeed happened on the last day of passenger services. If the substitute was a steam engine there could be problems with keeping to the timetable as turn round times were rather too tight for them.

Keith shed closed to steam on 30th June 1960 and although diesel locomotives would have appeared before that date the remaining goods trains were now all diesel worked. Types which appeared included English Electric Type 1 (Class 20), North British Type 2 (Class 21) and Derby or BRWC Type 2s (classes 24 and 26), with at least one appearance of an English Electric Type 4 (Class 40) when Aberlour was the terminus. An oddity was a Southern Region English Electric 0-6-0 shunter, No.15229, tried on Speyside freight services in 1959. This had a maximum speed of 27mpg but was not successful on the line.

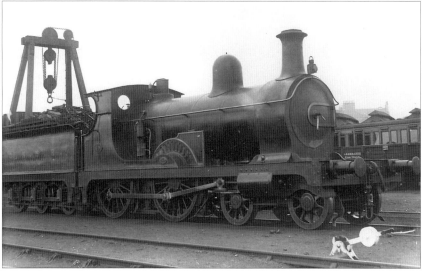

Class M was another type of Great North 4-4-0 used on the Speyside line. These locos dated from 1878; this one is in rebuilt condition.
(R K Blencowe)

Excursion Trains

Once the railway had been opened to Boat of Garten the possibilities of tourist traffic were recognised. Indeed the timetable for August 1866, the first for the complete line, advertised Tour No.2. Aberdeen - Dundee, Dundee - Perth, Perth - Boat of Garten via Dunkeld, Boat of Garten -Aberdeen via Keith, at a cost of 35/-. The Speyside scenery meant the line was a favourite for excursion trains and one of the first ran in connection with the Aberdeen autumn holiday in 1882 leaving Aberdeen at 8.20am and, after stops at suburban stations, was due into Grantown "about noon". The return journey began at 4.45pm with arrival in Aberdeen at "about 8pm". For this the travellers were charged 6/- First Class and 3/- Third Class.

For some years before the outbreak of war in 1914 great efforts were made to encourage this excursion trade. Regular special trains to Speyside began in June 1905, usually running on Wednesdays and Saturdays. At first they were non-stop to Craigellachie but later a call at Dufftown was included. The time taken to reach Boat of Garten (101¼ miles) was two and a half hours, very good going over a hilly route with many sharp curves and nearly half of which was single line. From the 1907 season those wanting to visit Tomintoul could use the railway owned bus from Ballindalloch. Later on arrangements were made for travellers to have a cold meal but, as the GNSR did not have restaurant cars, these had to be ordered in advance. The Company took considerable pride in the train and made great efforts to see it ran to time — and all for a return fare of 2/6. For a while during the Summer of 1908 the train worked through to Aviemore and on to Kingussie using the Great North engine and crew throughout for which the fares were 3/- and 4/- respectively. For some reason this did not prove popular and was not repeated.

It was not long before the Company realised that some members of the public were abusing this

A Speyside excursion from Aberdeen passes through wooded country near Knockando. The picture is from one of the numerous glass slides that the publicity conscious GNSR produced for use at 'Lantern Lectures' in the years before the Great War. *(GNSRA collection)*

Typical timings for the Strathspey Excursion are included in the working instructions issued for a summer Saturday in 1905. If demand was high, the train was run in two portions. Saloon carriages became available a few years later and were included in this train. Two of the tickets for this service are illustrated on page 81.

SATURDAY, 15th July

Keith Harvest Feeing Market; Inverurie and Keith Sales; Games at Elgin; Fast Excursion Train, Aberdeen to Strathspey and back; and Aberdeen Summer Holiday.

INVERURIE SALE.—10·22 a.m. Up Express Train is to call at Inverurie to lift Passengers for Aberdeen.

FAST EXCURSION TRAIN, ABERDEEN TO STRATHSPEY AND BACK.

Down Special Train. (Passengers.)				P.M.	Up Special and Altered Trains.			2·25 p.m. Goods Altered. P.M.	Passrs. P.M.
Aberdeen, depart	.	.	.	1 0					
Huntly	.	.	.	1*48	Boat of Garten, depart	.	2 25		8 0
Keith	.	..	.	2 *2	Nethybridge	.	.	2 40	5 9
Craigellachie	.	.	.	2 26	Grantown, arrive	.	.	2 55	—
Aberlour	.	..	.	2 32	Grantown, depart	.		4 5	8 18
Carron	.	.	.	2 37	Ballindalloch	.	.	4 45	8 36
Ballindalloch, arrive	.	.		2 49	Aberlour	.	.	5 34	8 52
Ballindalloch, depart	.	.		2*54	Craigellachie	.	.	5 40	9 E 3
Grantown	.	.	:	3 12	Keith	.	.	Stop	9*30
Nethybridge	.	.	.	3 21	Huntly	.	.	—	9*47
Boat of Garten, arrive	.	.		3 30	Aberdeen, arrive	.	.	—	10 40

* Passing time.   d Stops for crossing purposes only.   E Water Engine and Collect Tickets.

If 1·0 ᴘ.m. Down Special Train is run in duplicate, second portion is to follow a block behind the first portion to Craigellachie, where it is to be taken into Main Line Platform, and tickets of passengers in Train collected and Engine watered. It will be due to leave Craigellachie at 2·52 p.m., after crossing 1·15 p.m. Up Strathspey Train cross 2·25 p.m. Up Goods Train at Grantown, and arrive Boat of Garten at 3·52 p.m.

1·0 p.m. Down Special Train precedes 1·0 p.m. Down Denburn Goods Train from Aberdeen, 10·18 a.m. Down Goods Train from Grange, and crosses 1·15 p.m. Up Train at Carron, and 2·25 p.m. Up Goods Train (delayed) at Grantown. It is to take Passengers from Aberdeen for Craigellachie, Aberlour, Ballindalloch, Grantown, Nethybridge, and Boat of Garten.

2·25 p.m. Up Goods Train (altered from Grantown) crosses 1·0 p.m. Down Special and 3·15 p.m. Down Ordinary Trains at Grantown. Work and load to be regulated to enable Train to arrive Craigellachie at booked time.

8·0 p.m. Up Special Train crosses 6·30 p.m. Down Train at Boat of Garten and 7·0 p.m. Down Goods Train (delayed) at Ballindalloch. It is to take Passengers from Boat of Garten, Nethybridge, Grantown, Ballindalloch, Aberlour, and Craigellachie to Aberdeen.

These Trains will be formed of 1 Bogie Composite, 2 Corridor Thirds, 5 Thirds, and 2 Locker Brakes.

J. LOVIE to be Guard.

---

cheap excursion fare by travelling out to a Speyside station one Saturday and staying locally for two or three weeks. Meantime a friend in Aberdeen posted out another excursion ticket which was used for the return journey. To prevent this, tickets for the outward journey were marked with a special punch at the Aberdeen ticket barrier and when the excursion arrived back only tickets with this mark were accepted. Furthermore, no luggage was allowed.

The Speyside line played its part in the GNSR's 'Three Rivers Tour', first run in July 1907. Passengers left Aberdeen by rail for Dinnet, on the Deeside line, where they transferred to one of the Company's char-a-bancs which took them to Cockbridge at the head of Strathdon. At that time the road over the Lecht was considered unsuitable for motor vehicles so the stage on to Tomintoul was by privately owned horse drawn coach. Following an overnight stay in the village they completed the tour next day in another char-a-banc to Ballindalloch from where they returned by rail to Aberdeen.

After the Great War Speyside Excursions only ran occasionally but some were extended to give a circular tour going on via Aviemore to Perth and back via Forfar; the direction was sometimes reversed. Normally the same engines worked throughout and this brought Great North locos to Perth where they had to be turned for the homeward journey. From the mid-1930s until 1939, regular Saturday excursions from Aberdeen to Boat of Garten ran once again, complete with restaurant car, during July and August. These were included in the public timetable and could be used by any passengers. Occasional trains were resumed after the second World War, sometimes running only for private parties. What is believed to be the last such excursion ran on the Aberdeen Spring Holiday in 1961. The train departed Aberdeen at 10am and reached Kingussie at 1.50pm where it stayed for an hour. This was followed by a three hour stop at Pitlochry which was left at 7pm with arrival back in Aberdeen at 9.41pm. "Lunch will be served and finished before arrival at Kingussie and High Tea will be served at 7pm prompt." All this for £2/4/6d inclusive and certainly value for money.

Between 1933 and 1939, the line was also visited by the 'Northern Belle', an inclusive tour train operated by the LNER on several dates each summer from London. This was aimed at the wealthy traveller, the fare being £20, but for that they had accommodation on the train and meals either on board or at suitable hotels, plus various excursions.

Saturday 25th March 1967 saw what must have been the biggest train ever to run on Speyside when British Rail ran a 'Grand Scottish Tour' from Edinburgh back to Edinburgh via Carlisle, Aberdeen, Craigellachie and Aviemore. This had no less than 18 coaches, weighed in at over 600 tons and took 1 hour 25 minutes for the journey from Craigellachie to Boat of Garten, only 17 minutes more than the rail-bus. Appropriately, the last passenger working over the line was, as previously mentioned, a GNSR Association special train.

Excursion trains were not the only way in which the railways directly catered for holiday makers. Starting in 1933 the LNER equipped some old coaches to act as Camping Coaches and these proved very popular. Two were located on Speyside. Cromdale was first on the scene having one from 1935-39 while Aberlour also had one in 1939 and both had them for the 1954 and 1955 seasons. It is surprising that Speyside was not more popular with holiday makers.

Two Class D40s ready to leave Boat of Garten with a circular tour from Aberdeen via Perth, the Highland main line and the Speyside line. The train consists of LMS stock but the LNER locomotives hauled the train from Perth. A complicated shunt was required at Boat of Garten as it was not possible to run directly on to the Speyside line at that time. (F R Hebron/J L Stevenson collection)

Two photos of staff at Ballindalloch, above during the First World War – a 'Defence of the Realm' poster can be seen in the background – and below about 1922. With most able bodied men away, a female clerkess was employed during the War. In the 1923 photograph, the staff were identified as, back row from left, shunter (name not known), Sam Mearns (driver at Boat of Garten), John Ross (signalman), Angus McPherson (foreman) and R Wood (signalman); front row J McNaughton (goods clerk), Charles Murray (goods clerk), R Gordon (Station Master), W Wood (goods checker) and W Morrison (passenger clerk). Messrs Gordon, R Wood and W Wood appear in both. Both photos were taken before fire damaged the station building.

The Railwaymen

In the early days the Strathspey line stations provided employment for 18 people, nine of whom were Stationmasters, or Agents. They received £45 per year apart from those at Grantown and Abernethy who received £50. Each station also had a clerk whose rates ranged between £20 and £30 while the pointsmen at Aberlour, Grantown and Abernethy were paid 15/- per week.

Among these first appointments, the *Elgin Courant* was particularly pleased to note, was James Barron, driver of the Speyside Coach, appointed Agent at Grantown. "His selection is a judicious one for his local knowledge is complete, and a more steady and trustworthy man could not have been found." Another experienced man, J M Stewart, was in charge at Craigellachie having moved from Drummuir Station, while one of the guards was a Mr McKenzie from the Strathisla Railway.

Forty years later the traffic staff had increased to 35. By then the Stationmasters' salaries ranged from £60 at Blacksboat, Advie and Nethy Bridge to £82 at Ballindalloch, the highest amount paid to any stationmaster on the GNSR branch lines. By then only Advie did not have a clerk but their pay varied widely. At Blacksboat, where no doubt a youth was employed, it was £15 but the senior clerk at Aberlour received £60. Signalmen were paid £47 to £52 with porters getting £44 to £47. Each station had a cleaner who normally received 1/- per week. The Locomotive Department employed 3 drivers and firemen with an extra crew for 13 weeks. Drivers were paid 5/8 to 6/6 per day and firemen 3/10. The two full time engine cleaners at Boat of Garten received 2/8 to 2/10 per day and again an extra man was employed for 13 weeks.

At first staff were expected to find their own accommodation locally but in time the Company realised the need to provide permanently available housing and constructed dwellings for the Agents as well as a number of smaller ones for other staff. These were nearly always built in stone, although a wooden building at Nethy Bridge sufficed for the crossing keeper.

It is well known that working hours in the 19th century were long and arduous and this is borne out in the Board of Trade report on a fairly minor derailment that occurred to the 4pm Up mixed train in May 1888. The driver and fireman had booked on duty at Boat of Garten at 4.10am and were due to finish their day's work at 9.30pm "or a little sooner". The next day their hours would be 9.10am until 6pm. The Inspecting Officer was scathing. "The evidence in this case discloses the fact that the hours of work of some of the servants of the Great North of Scotland Company upon the Speyside section are far too long. The driver and fireman work for 17 hours 20 minutes on one day and 8 hours 50 minutes on the next, and the guard for 15 hours on one day and 6 hours on the next. Even the average of two days in the case of the driver and fireman is too high, but it is positively dangerous for such men to work over 17 hours on any one day, and under no circumstances should they be allowed to do so no matter what may be their hours on the following day." The directors heeded the warning and instructed the Locomotive Superintendent to look into the hours of duty of his men, especially those referred to in the Report.

After 1919, when the 8 hour working day was introduced, more staff were needed working complex shift arrangements. A set of engine and train crew diagrams for the winter timetable for 1948/49 has survived and this gives a picture of how the line was operated in the steam age. All the trains were diagrammed for Great North 4-4-0 engines of which two were based at Boat of Garten and crews swapped engines each day. The engine diagrams were :

Boat Turn 1 – complete passenger service of three trains each way to Craigellachie. The late Saturday train was worked separately.

Boat Turn 2 – three day cycle consisting of :

 Mondays and Thursdays : 8.30am Goods from Boat of Garten to Elgin, 5.8pm Elgin to Lossiemouth and 5.33pm back to Elgin.

 Tuesdays and Fridays : 6.5am Goods from Elgin to Keith via Craigellachie, 3.50pm Passenger from Cairnie to Elgin via Buckie, Light Engine to Keith.

 Wednesdays : 12.25pm Goods from Keith to Boat of Garten.

 Saturdays : 12.25pm Goods from Keith to Craigellachie and, if required, a trip at 2.20pm to Knockando and return. Finally 9.45pm passenger train to Boat of Garten.

Elgin Turn 1 – similar to Boat Turn 2 including

 Tuesdays and Fridays : 12.25pm Goods from Keith to Boat of Garten

 Wednesdays and Saturdays : 8.30am Goods Boat of Garten to Elgin

Keith Turn 9 – including

 Mondays and Thursdays : 12.25pm from Keith to Boat of Garten

 Tuesdays and Fridays : 8.30am from Boat of Garten.

The remaining Goods trains, the 5.55am from Keith to Boat of Garten and the 2.45pm from Boat of Garten to Keith, were worked by Keith Turn 4 engine on a daily out and home basis. Likewise the Tuesday and Friday only working for outward whisky at 10.30am from Keith to Ballindalloch and the 2.25pm return were worked by Keith Turn 8 engine and men.

The enginemen's workings were somewhat simpler than those for the engines. The goods trains from Boat of Garten at 8.30am and 2.45pm were worked by a double shifted diagram booking on at 6.55am and 1.50pm. These men changed footplates at Ballindalloch with the Elgin men and Keith men working the 5.50am and the 12.25pm (SX) ex Keith respectively.

As with the locomotives the extra train at 9.45pm from Craigellachie on Saturdays engendered complications to the enginemen's diagrams. The two passenger shifts (Turn 1) booked on later at 7.15am and 4.30pm. This allowed the first shift to work the 12.52pm from Boat of Garten and the 3.0pm return from Craigellachie normally worked by the second shift, albeit at the cost of an extended shift of 9 hours 15 minutes. The second shift of Turn 1 then worked the 4.50pm passenger as far as Knockando where they changed footplates with the Turn 2 (second shift) men working the 2.45pm Goods from Boat of Garten to Craigellachie. The Turn 2 men off the Goods then worked the passenger train forward to Craigellachie, returning with the 6.45pm passenger train to Boat of Garten. Meantime the Turn 1 men followed on with the 2.45pm Goods arriving at Craigellachie at 7.8pm where they changed footplates with the Keith men on the 12.25pm Goods from Keith (which terminated at Craigellachie on Saturdays) and then finished their week by working the 9.45pm 'Boozer' back to Boat of Garten. The object of the Saturday changes to the diagrams was, of course, to keep the additional hours within acceptable limits.

It can be seen that Boat of Garten Shed required 4 sets of enginemen, 4 drivers and 4 firemen, to operate the train service. During the staff holiday season additional staff would have been provided and during the rest of the year relief would have been supplied from Keith Shed. Later Aviemore shed would also have provided relief staff.

The number of staff at Boat of Garten did not warrant a full time shedmaster and supervision was exercised by the 'Driver in Charge' who received a small wage increment for his extra responsibilities. The driver in charge, and presumably his fireman, did enjoy a 'steady' shift being permanently on the early passenger shift. The remaining three shifts rotated weekly in turn. There were also 2 shed labourers, one working overnight. These two posts enjoyed a 30 minute meal break and changed shifts weekly. The shed labourers' duties included assisting to coal engines and cleaning and lighting up engines. There were 4 guards based at Boat of Garten and their workings were very similar to those described for the engine crews.

Whisky

When the business of distilling became legal in 1823 a number of distilleries were connected to or owned by the larger farms in the area. This had benefits, such as a local market for barley, but in particular it provided work for farm labourers in the winter months. Production is not a continuous process; it is seasonal and this brought peaks and troughs with goods traffic increasing in the autumn, winter and spring months. Tuesdays and Thursdays were "whisky making days" when wagons were collected from the various stills. Deliveries of coal to fuel the distilleries and grain were made daily. The cold frosty days of winter were perhaps the best with a fall of snow to keep the water temperature low, ideal for distilling, but not so good for the railway. Signalmen wired Aberdeen every day between 3 and 4 o'clock to give a weather report to ensure services kept running.

When the water supply lessened in the spring, grain stocks became exhausted and the requirement for draff, a distillery by-product used for cattle food, lessened as stock returned to the fields. The "Silent Season" descended over the distilleries. From May to October the workers returned to the fields and coppersmiths, carpenters and painters carried out maintenance.

Imperial, Knockando (which was ¾ mile north of the station of that name) and Tamdhu (at Knockando station) had private sidings but Dailuaine and Balmenach were too far from the railway to be served in this way and built their own lines while others such as Cardhu and Cragganmore used the sidings at Knockando and Ballindalloch respectively.

In the Spring of 1885 Messrs McKenzie were considering a railway from their Dailuaine distillery, which lay about ¾ mile off the line, to join it about ½ mile east of Carron. For some reason this scheme, although agreed by the Great North, went into abeyance but was revived in 1893. Even then nothing further happened and it was not until 1905 that agreement was finally reached and the siding and associated connection were laid in.

At Cromdale the owners of Balmenach Distillery, Messrs John McGregor & Sons, also felt improved communication was required over the intervening 1½ miles to the station. Their line was opened in 1897 but whereas at Dailuaine the connection was direct with the running line, at Cromdale it was made via a siding in the station yard. Messrs McGregor bought their engine from Aveling Porter and being based on the maker's well known traction engines, it had a flywheel. It was not long before the owners decided to make fuller use of their new acquisition and employ it to drive the distillery machinery even though an extra siding was needed to allow this. The engine survived until 1936 when it was replaced by a standard 0-4-0 saddle tank engine from Andrew Barclay, a well known firm of locomotive builders in Kilmarnock.

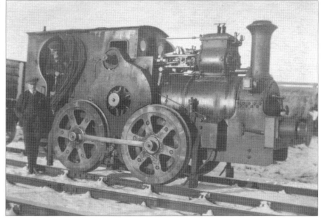

An Aveling Porter of the type used at Balmenach - the photo may even have been taken there. It was succeeded by the 0-4-0 saddle tank shown on page 69. (Bill Emslie collection)

From *Wort, Worms and Washbacks, Memoirs from the Stillhouse* by John McDougall and Gavin D Smith. Neil Wilson Publishing Ltd, Glasgow, 1999. The writer is John McDougall, Assistant Manager at Dailuaine

Dailuaine is situated just a couple of miles along the Spey valley from Imperial Distillery and it nestles in a little wooded hollow. Looking at the distillery today there is a lot of flat, empty ground around the plant that was all rail sidings when I was there. The railway ran just behind the distillery, and as at Balmenach, it brought in malt and coal. The railway was a great feature of Dailuaine, and we had our own little puggie engine which shunted wagons of barley and malt around. There was a spur line off the Strathspey railway line near Imperial Distillery, and the puggie would go down there to pick up wagons dropped off by the main line train. The engine driver was called Willie Wilson and was known as Puggie Wull. He used to 'go with the moon' as they say and at certain times he was likely to just drive the engine at you if you were in his way. ....

The puggie engine was quite a feature of Dailuaine and we even got train spotters coming to photograph it from time to time. One day we were approached by Lui, a French magazine we had never heard of, which wanted to use the engine in a photo shoot with some fashion models. I was put in charge of organising the event, and Puggie Wull got the engine all polished up for the day. The crew duly turned up with the girls wearing full length fur coats on what I thought was quite a mild day. Soft French lassies, I thought. 'Are you wearing those coats because you're feeling the cold?' I asked one of them. She smiled at me and pulled her coat open to reveal that she was completely naked underneath. The girls from the distillery thought this was absolutely disgusting and went and locked themselves in their office. As they were retreating, I noticed that the men were leaving their posts in great haste, abandoning the stillhouse, the maltings, the dried soubles plant and every other bit of distillery to come and watch. Geordie Davidson, who worked in the cooperage, was so excited by this turn of events that he pulled a cask from the bottom of the pile in error, and the rest of the heap rolled all over the yard. A few even ended up in the burn and found their way into the Spey.

My wife chose that precise moment to walk into the yard to see what all the fuss was about. My protestations that nobody told me that Lui was that sort of publication were clearly not believed. There were some long silences at home that evening. This was the swinging sixties, but nothing much swung around the Aberlour area – at least not until that day – so the excitement and outrage (according to gender) was not surprising. A while after all this happened, we did get to see the published photographs in Lui, and I have to admit it was quite a good feature. When we showed the pictures to Puggie Wull he studied them carefully for a while, then said, "Aye, the engine looks well, right enough."

Dailuaine also had its own 'pug', again a Barclay 0-4-0 tank, which came second-hand in 1906 and lasted until 1939. Its replacement, this time bought new, was yet another standard Barclay similar to that at Balmenach. To begin with the Great North worked the traffic between the exchange siding and Carron but in 1913 the Dailuaine engine joined that select band of industrial locomotives authorised to work on main lines, in this case only as far as Carron and the siding to Imperial Distillery. This was the only place on the old GNSR system where a signalman acted as a guard. This additional duty came about when Dailuaine Distillery contacted the signal box on one of those old style "wind-up" phones and asked for the duty signalman to come "doon" with the tablet to send a train of wagons from Dailuaine ground frame to the yard at Carron. The signalman took out the Aberlour to Carron tablet and walked down the single line to Dailuaine ground frame where the Pug was waiting. He would unlock the frame with the tablet and let the engine and its train of wagons out onto the main line and then close up the frame again. During the shunting at

Carron yard and the Imperial Distillery (where the Carron/Knockando tablet was required to release the ground frame) the signalman looked after the interests of the train and then escorted it back along the line to Dailuaine. This distillery Pug was allowed to work for a short distance in the Aberlour direction when the Dailuaine filter beds needed attention, although in this case it had to be accompanied by the Carron stationmaster in person.

When either of the distillery pugs were not available, motive power was hired from British Railways. For instance Z4 0-4-2T No.68191, normally used on Aberdeen docks, was hired to Dailuaine in 1957.

Both the Barclays continued at work until the railway closed, with the honour of being the last steam

Loading a 54 gallon hogshead at Knockando Distillery siding in the 1960s. (Aberdeen Journals)

locomotive to work on the Speyside line going to the pug *Balmenach* when it was driven from its home distillery to the engine shed at Dailuaine distillery on 31st October 1968. The locomotive remained at that location until 3rd July 1977 when it was transported to Aviemore; it is now at Boat of Garten awaiting restoration. The Dailuaine engine required extensive overhaul and after many years at the Strathspey Railway it was moved in 1994 to Aberfeldy Distillery where it was cosmetically restored and put on static display as part of the Dewars World of Whisky Attraction.

Although it did not have its own siding at Ballindalloch, Cragganmore made history in 1887 when it despatched the first block train load of whisky. This went to Dundee, at that time an important centre for blending.

The distilleries not only provided outward traffic by the despatch of whisky and draff, there were also considerable inward loads. Dailuaine, for example, is recorded as having been responsible for a combined total of no less than 10,665 tons in 1904 — and that without any rail connection. During February 1909 the siding at Knockando Distillery handled 317 tons. Draff was sent to Cove, Cults, Kittybrewster and Inverness — 96 tons in all. This was for use as cattle food and necessitated clean open wagons as the last thing a farmer wanted was "his coo's chewing coal." Whisky (sadly the quantity is not recorded!) went to Edinburgh and Glasgow with the barrels returning empty. Several stations on the line to Inverness delivered 128 tons of barley with 87 tons of coal and 10½ tons of coke also arriving to say nothing of various other small items. Finally, the Great North's costing exercise

Not from the pens of Messrs McDougall and Smith but from that famous poet 'Anon' come the following immortal lines:

> The Lord's my Shepherd, I'll not want,
> As long as there's whisky in Glen Grant,
> But when it's done; none left to pour,
> I'll up the line to Cragganmore.

It is likely that this little piece of doggerel dates from the very early days of the railway. One thing is sure, the poet had a very discriminating taste in whisky. Glen Grant is of course at Rothes and Cragganmore is the famous establishment adjacent to Ballindalloch station.

for 1902/3 shows over 65,000 tons of goods and minerals forwarded from Speyside stations, the bulk of which must have come from this source.

There is evidence that road transport was beginning to make inroads on the traffic by the mid-1920s. Loss of inter-distillery movement of stocks is noted as is the short-haul to the harbour at Buckie for loading on to ships belonging to Coast Lines.

LNER records for 1938 show that the five stations serving the distilleries received 2,300 tons of mineral traffic, 18,100 tons of higher rated merchandise and 17,000 tons of coal. Outward business amounted to 5,600 tons of minerals and 8,400 tons of merchandise which of course included whisky. In other words these stations between them accounted for about 87% of the traffic handled on the branch during that year.

Despite the gradual loss of traffic to road, whisky played a very large part in the life of the Speyside line but the railway staff were only human and many stories have been told. Some of the best were related by Maurice Shand who undertook relief work at several stations on Speyside in the early part of a railway career which finished as stationmaster at Glasgow Central. "I was asked to examine a load of whisky wagons to detect broaching, i.e. tampering of the casks. They were most ingenious fellows — some of the porters at the distillery stations. They broached the whisky casks and then covered up the penetration of the cask with a material which made it well nigh impossible to distinguish that it had been interfered with. Witness the notorious case where whisky leaking was carried out in a goods shed under the very nose of a detective from the Police Department. The stationmaster was demoted to a smaller station, as was his successor."

The techniques used by the railwaymen are illustrated in this story, from the 1950s, related by a railwayman from Elgin who was sent as relief to one of the Speyside stations and introduced to the practices. "My fellow railwaymen at this location all seemed fairly happy 'chiels,' except for the stationmaster. He was dressed in regulation railway uniform complete with full-length coat and peaked cap. Initially I put this down to the fact that during the war he had served in the navy. I assumed that he still pictured himself on the deck of his destroyer in a Force 10 in the middle of the Atlantic, rather than in charge of a peaceful Speyside railway station.

"Whisky was gathered from various distilleries and sent south on Tuesdays and Thursdays. The railway lorry arrived and as we began loading operations the stationmaster appeared. 'Anything good boys' he queried? By anything good he meant whisky filled sherry casks; these were set aside for inspection. One of the straw filled sacks used in the loading process was placed in front of the chosen barrel. The stationmaster removed his full-length coat, on the inside lining was a pocket that contained a small tool kit. What followed resembled the procedure used in a hospital operation.

First item called for was the hand drill. The request was repeated by the railwayman handing over the instrument. When the cask was drilled, the

At Balmenach, the bonded warehouse was just short of the distillery, so trains stopped for barrels to be loaded via this overhead crane. Photographed on 20th June 1967. (John M Boyes/ Armstrong Railway Trust)

The Dailuaine Distillery pug shunting a couple of wagons at Carron.
(R K Blencowe)

stationmaster blew into the hole. This was to put some pressure inside the barrel so the whisky would flow freely. Apparently, if you did not do this the whisky would just dribble down the side of the cask, which was useless for bottling purposes. A later version of the hand drill had a copper tube incorporated into the handle to speed up discharge operations. Bottles used for storing the whisky were the old screw top lemonade type. It was the procedure to take two bottles from a Butt, which was the large size of cask and one from the smaller hogshead.

"Next up in the operations was the 'spile', a thin piece of tapered wood that looked a little like an anorexic pencil, which was used to plug the hole in the cask. The protruding end of this bit of wood was cut off with a junior hacksaw. At all times the request for each bit of kit was repeated by the railwayman handing it over. Each item on return was replaced back into the internal pocket of the stationmaster's coat. With the 'spile' in place a request was made for some 'black sh##e' which was a handful of soil from the loading bank. This was rubbed over the operation site until it matched the rest of the cask.

"Last procedure was the 'watertight test'. The cask was tipped and held at an angle to ensure that the wound was completely closed up with no leak or sign of weeping. On this inspection being successfully passed the cask was loaded onto the wagon. Nobody really seemed to bother about this whisky acquiring activity, that was until an incident up the line."

However, it would be maligning the Speyside staff to imagine that such nefarious work was peculiar to some of them -– far from it. At one period thieves became so skilful at boring into barrels through the floors of wagons sitting in sidings en-route to Aberdeen that whisky trains were run non-stop directly into the secure Caledonian Railway yard at Guild Street.

After closure, the Dailuaine pug sat outside its shed and was photographed early in 1969 after a heavy snowfall.
(Richard Martin/GNSRA)

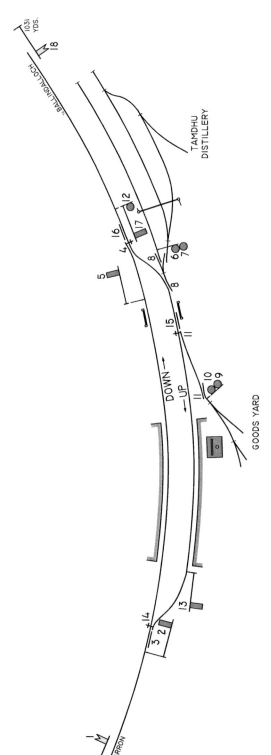

The signalling at Knockando was typical of all the crossing stations on the line. Distant, home and starting signals were provided in each direction, all controlled from a single box which also contained the token instruments. There were 18 working levers and no spares. (Drawing by Robert Dey based on official information)

On the other hand the signal box was a later design. By the time the station opened, the Great North had adopted a contemporary design with more pronounced features, but still in wood. The 'Tamdhu' nameboard reflects the use of the station as the distillery visitor centre. (Keith Fenwick)

Signalling

For the first thirty years or so the Speyside line was worked in accordance with the Company's Rules which allowed only one train on each section of the single line. As was the case on the rest of its system, train movements were controlled by telegraph communication between the stations. Out of course crossing of trains and operation of trains not in the timetable were authorised by telegram from Aberdeen. When the line was extended to Boat of Garten the Inspecting Officer recommended that additional instruments be provided between Nethybridge and Boat of Garten but apparently this was never done.

Although in 1863 the Inspecting Officer noted only one passing place, at Speyside Junction (later Craigellachie), another must have been installed at Ballindalloch not long afterwards as the 1866 timetable shows trains crossing there.

A loop was provided at Carron in 1884 but little else changed until the Company was forced to bring its working into line with the requirements of the Regulation of Railways Act, 1889. This called for signals and points to be interlocked so that they worked in conjunction with each other; also for each driver on a single line to be in possession of a token giving his train the sole right to occupy the line between signal boxes. Because the Great North had to resignal nearly all its lines, implementation of this Act took some time.

Interlocking and new signals were provided at Ballindalloch in 1892. Other major changes followed in 1894 starting in January with a loop at Grantown. Later in that year token working was introduced with block stations at Carron, Ballindalloch and Grantown. The sidings at intermediate stations were released by the token for the respective section. A further loop and block post was provided at Dalbeallie (Knockando) in 1899. Following the increase in traffic consigned south through Boat of Garten, loops were provided at Cromdale in 1907 and Aberlour three years later, both becoming block stations. Although all signals were initially lower quadrant the LNER (and later BR) progressively converted them to upper quadrant, except for the up distant at Aberlour and all those at Ballindalloch. Initially Tyer's No 6 tablet was installed for all block sections but this was later replaced by Tyer's Key Token.

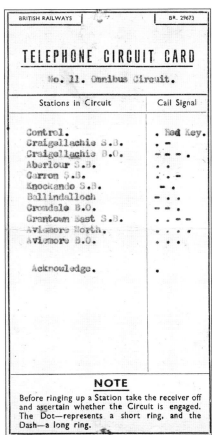

Loop capacities were as follows plus one engine and brakevan in each case :

Aberlour	32 wagons
Carron	21 wagons
Knockando	28 wagons
Ballindalloch	15 wagons
Cromdale	Not recorded
Grantown (East)	26 wagons

On most railways the single line token was exchanged between signalman and engine crew by hand, with obvious dangers when done on the move. In the late 1880s the Great North's Locomotive Superintendent, James Manson, developed an apparatus by which this could be done safely by non-stopping trains and all the Speyside signal boxes, except those at Ballindalloch and Cromdale, were provided with it about twenty years later.

Apart from Cromdale signal box, which closed in 1921 when the loop was removed, the other boxes were operational until all traffic ceased south of Aberlour on 4th November 1968. Even then they remained nominally open until 15th December to allow the signalmen to work out their notice.

Finally, mention should be made of the signalling at Boat of Garten so far as it affected Speyside trains. The actual junction between the two companies was originally only at the south end of the station. Another connection was installed at the north end in 1907. But even so, trains to and from Craigellachie could only use the eastern platform face furthest from the main buildings. Through trains from the Aviemore direction had to draw forward at Boat of Garten towards Grantown-on-Spey West, for which the relevant token had to be issued, before reversing into the main southbound platform from where they could set off for the Speyside line. This continued until another cross-over was provided in 1958 to allow the railbus to operate through from Aviemore. Under this scheme the double track to Tullochgorum could have disappeared as there was a serious proposal to make a fully signalled junction there complete with signal box.

Up starter at Ballindalloch, one of the Great North lower quadrants to survive until closure in 1968.

(Keith Fenwick)

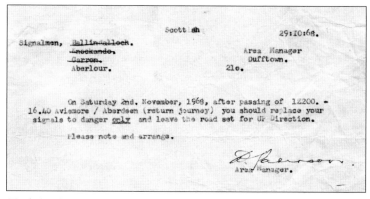

Final circular to signalmen instructing them to leave the points set for trains to run from Aviemore but to leave all the signals at danger.

Railways That Might Have Been

Early Optimists

The railway might have come earlier to part of Strathspey if any of the three grandiose schemes for railways connecting Inverness with Perth promoted in 1845 during the Railway Mania had been built.

The **Direct Northern Railway** would have connected the Scottish Midland Junction Railway, later part of the Caledonian Railway, at Coupar Angus, between Perth and Forfar, with Elgin, thence via the proposed line from there to Inverness. It would have required a mile long tunnel under the boundary between Perthshire and Aberdeenshire and a branch would have run from Tomintoul via Mortlach (Dufftown) to Keith.

The **Perth & Northern Counties Railway** was also based on Coupar Angus but its route was to be via Blairgowrie, Braemar and Inchrory, then along the valleys of the Avon, the Livet and down Glenrinnes to Dufftown where it would split. One line would go to Keith and the other connect with the Morayshire Railway at Rothes and so on to Elgin.

Finally the **Great Northern Central Railway** proposed to run from Perth via Dunkeld, Braemar, Tomintoul, Ballindalloch, Craigellachie and Rothes to Elgin.

On a more local basis the **Banffshire Railway** was promoted to link Dufftown with Portgordon on the Moray Firth. This line, which would have gone via Keith and Fochabers, was intended to provide an outlet not only for agricultural produce but also the output of the ironstone mines in the area and was promoted in connection with a from Aberdeen to Elgin via Banff and the Moray Firth coast.

None of these proposals progressed any further but the lure of the iron ore lingered on for at least a further 80 years. As already related the Morayshire Railway a few years later had its own ideas for a route south.

Highland Rivalry

Moving on to the early 1880s, two railways were promoted, both affecting Nethy Bridge but unlikely to have had much of an impact on the Speyside line itself. To understand this it is necessary to give some background to the antagonism and marked lack of co-operation between the Great North and Highland Railways.

The two Companies met at Elgin, Keith and Boat of Garten and while comparatively little traffic would be exchanged at Boat, Keith and Elgin were a different matter. Traditionally exchange had been done at Keith and had been recognised in an 1865 Act of Parliament. It meant, of course, that the Highland had the greater share of the income from through traffic to Inverness. However in 1880 the GNSR had a new general manager who was determined to get a bigger share for his Company. The Highland naturally opposed any change and the Great North sought ways of overcoming the situation.

The Highland had a monopoly of all traffic to and from Inverness which obviously it was keen to retain and consequently the directors were very disturbed when a new route from Glasgow, which would approach Inverness via the Great Glen, was proposed. In return for the Great North's undertaking not to support this, the Highland agreed that some of the traffic between Aberdeen and Inverness would in future be exchanged at Elgin and went on to propose its new direct route between Aviemore and Inverness via Carrbridge, thus avoiding the detour taken by the existing main line via Boat of Garten and Forres.

When the Great North directors considered this they decided that as it would not provide any interchange facilities with the Speyside line the latter should be extended from Boat of Garten to Carrbridge with the railway north of there being a joint venture. Needless to say the Highland rejected the idea and this led the Great North to undertake a survey of their own route from Nethy Bridge to Inverness. This promptly made the Highland rescind the recent exchange agreement.

On the face of it the Great North directors were apparently willing to spend a large sum of money connecting one of their rural branches with Inverness. However at the same time a group of North-east lairds put forward their own proposal for the **Strathspey, Strathdon & Deeside Junction Railway** connecting Cambus O'May, on Deeside, with Nethy Bridge. This 40 mile line going via Boultenstone and Allargue would pass through virtually uninhabited countryside but would ostensibly tap traffic from granite quarries as well as iron ore deposits known to exist in the area. It would have had a summit level of about 1,500 feet, four tunnels and stiff gradients such as the 4 miles at 1 in 50 to 55 facing eastbound trains leaving the Spey valley. Combined, these two proposals apparently offered an alternative route from Aberdeen to Inverness but when their respective Bills came before Parliament in 1884, members had little difficulty in rejecting both.

The main benefit of all this to the Great North was to expose how unfairly the Highland treated the Inverness to Aberdeen traffic, so much so that when the latter's Bill for the direct line north from Aviemore was published it contained a clause allowing traffic to be exchanged at both Keith and Elgin.

Many years later correspondence between William Ferguson, the Great North chairman, and his general manager, William Moffat, came to light which revealed a much deeper reason behind the Carrbridge proposal. It would have formed the final link in their dream of a railway connecting Dundee with Inverness entirely under GNSR ownership. This would have run from Dundee to Boat of Garten via Ballater and then on through Carrbridge. Strangely enough, following a private conversation between Ferguson and his opposite number John Walker on the North British Railway, the latter apparently gave serious consideration to the proposal.

The guard opens the gates at Nethy Bridge for the railbus to pass. If one of the abortive schemes had come about, this would have been the starting point of a line through to Inverness. (Graham Maxtone collection)

The Lure of Iron Ore

Deposits of iron ore around the Lecht had long excited the interest of local people and this was indeed noted when prospects for the Speyside Railway were originally considered. High hopes were raised by an analysis done in Glasgow but in the end it was found that it could not compete on Teeside with Spanish ore; even so the prospect of exploitation remained in peoples' minds.

The mid-1890s saw a serious attempt to add the Tomintoul district to the rail network. Much livestock was reared on the uplands and had to be driven to market. Similarly The Glenlivet Distillery was faced with the cost of double handling much of its raw materials to say nothing of the whisky itself— and still there were hopes of working that iron ore.

There were two obvious routes for the line. One started at Dufftown and went via Glen Rinnes. Needless to say the inhabitants of Dufftown were greatly in favour as they could see it enhancing the town's role as a market centre. The other possibility followed the valley of the Avon from Ballindalloch — a route preferred by the townsfolk of Grantown who feared they would otherwise lose much of the trade they currently did with the area. Having calculated that they would lose some £800 a year if the traffic was diverted to Dufftown, the Great North directors preferred the Ballindalloch proposal which would be both shorter and more easily graded.

Much of the land for the first option passed through the Duke of Richmond's estates and negotiations with his representatives proceeded on the basis that as the railway was estimated to run at a loss, the owners and tenants might be asked to make this up. The Duke however preferred to sell the land at favourable terms rather than be involved in unpredictable losses. The Ballindalloch route would be largely on land belonging to Sir George Macpherson Grant, a director of the Highland Railway, who reckoned that, for various reasons, he and his tenants would gain little from it. He was therefore not prepared to subscribe to the capital costs nor to donate the land but equally he would not raise outright opposition.

Locally feelings ran high but whatever the rights and wrongs of it all nothing happened for the usual reason of lack of willingness by the inhabitants to support their desires with hard cash.

Even so, the GNSR did not entirely give up and sent further samples of the ore for analysis in 1909 and again two years later, only to have the poor quality confirmed once more.

Astonishing as it may seem, the London & North Eastern Railway, as successor to the Great North, found itself embroiled when it was approached by a speculator called Macdonald suggesting that a railway was all that was required to produce riches for both parties. Plans were developed and further samples tested but with much the same result as before. Not only so, but Mr Macdonald became very elusive. The file was eventually closed on 9th June 1928.

To-day the observant traveller on the road between Tomintoul and the Lecht will see, on the left hand side just before the steep part of the climb begins at the Well of Lecht, a ruined stone building about half a mile up Coire Buidhe — all that remains of brave proposals to mine iron ore in this remote area.

Appendix 1 : Opening and Closing Dates

Name	Dist	Opened	Closed Passenger	Goods
Craigellachie (a)	0	1 Jul 1863	6 May 1968	4 Nov 1968
Aberlour	2¾	1 Jul 1863	18 Oct 1965	15 Nov 1971
Dailuaine Halt	4¾	18 Nov 1933	18 Oct 1965	—
Dailuaine Distillery (b)	5	1905	—	4 Nov 1968
Carron	5½	1 Jul 1863	18 Oct 1965	4 Nov 1968
Imperial Distillery (c)	5¾	1897	—	4 Nov 1968
Imperial Cottages Halt	6	15 Jun 1959	18 Oct 1965	
Knockando House (d)	7	1869	18 Oct 1965	—
Knockando Distillery (c)	7¾	16 Oct 1905	—	4 Nov 1968
Gilbey's Cottages Halt	8	15 Jun 1959	18 Oct 1965	
Knockando (e)	8¼	1 Jul 1899	18 Oct 1965	4 Nov 1968
Blacksboat	10½	1 Jul 1863	18 Oct 1965	2 Nov 1959
Ballindalloch	12¼	1 Jul 1863	18 Oct 1965	4 Nov 1968
Advie (1st location)	14½	1 Jul 1863	1 Sep 1868	1 Sep 1868
Advie (2nd location)	15¼	1 Sep 1868	18 Oct 1965	2 Nov 1959
Dalvey	17¼	1 Jul 1863	1 Sep 1868	1 Sep 1868
Dalvey Farm Halt	17½	15 Jun 1959	18 Oct 1965	—
Cromdale	21¼	1 Jul 1863	18 Oct 1965	4 Nov 1968
Grantown–on-Spey (f)	24¼	1 Jul 1863	18 Oct 1965	4 Nov 1968
Ballifurth Farm Halt	26¾	15 Jun 1959	18 Oct 1965	—
Nethy Bridge (g)	28¾	1 Jul 1863	18 Oct 1965	25 Jan 1965
Boat of Garten (h)	33½	1 Aug 1866	18 Oct 1965	2 Nov 1965

Notes

(a) Called Strathspey Junction until 1 June 1864.

(b) Exchange sidings for Dailuaine Distillery.

(c) Private siding.

(d) Private station for passengers only. Called Knockando until 2 October 1905.

(e) Opened as Tamdhu Siding 29 May 1896. Renamed Dalbeallie and opened for all traffic 1 Jul 1899. Renamed Knockando 2 October 1905. Private sidings for Tamdhu Distillery were off station yard.

(f) Grantown until 1 June 1912. Renamed Grantown-on-Spey (East) in 1949 or 1950.

(g) Called Abernethy until December 1867.

(h) Highland Railway station, opened 3 August 1863. Dates shown are for GNSR traffic.

Timber Sidings

A siding was authorised at Pollowick, about 1½ miles north of Cromdale, in August 1867, for timber from Lord Seafield's estate. Closure date unknown.

Four sidings were laid in to handle the large amount of timber felled on Speyside during and shortly after the Great War. These were :

(i) Knockando, 850 yards on the Carron side of Knockando station. Authorised 1917, closure date unknown.

(ii) Ballindalloch, ³/₈ mile north of Ballindalloch station. Opened January 1920. Closed June 1930.

(iii) Nethy Bridge, 250 yards north of Nethy Bridge station. Opened July 1917. Closed April 1920.

(iv) Abernethy, ¾ mile beyond Nethy Bridge station. Opened July 1918. Closed September 1923.

Appendix 2 : Traffic

Source : GNSR and LNER papers.

Year ended 31st July 1865   Strathspey Railway

	Number	Income
Passengers - 1st class	11,103	£456
- 3rd and Excursion	22,962	£701
- Parliamentary	63,579	£1,406
Total Passengers	**97,644**	
Carriages and Horses		£31
Mails		£200
Goods, Minerals and Livestock		£1,892
Tolls payable by Keith and Dufftown Rly for use of Balvenie Extension*		£1,129
Other		£24
Total		**£5,839**
Working expenses		£6,674
Operating loss		**£835**

* The line between Dufftown and Craigellachie was legally part of the Strathspey Railway.

Year ended 31st July 1903   Great North of Scotland Railway

Passengers

Passengers Booked	Number	Income
Between station on Speyside	56,871	£1,898
To and from stations beyond Speyside	44,483	£2,396
Throughout between Craigellachie and Boat of Garten	440	£108
	101,794	£4,402
Season tickets	721	£150
Parcels		£801
Total		**£5,353**

Goods, Minerals and Livestock

Consigned	Livestock (trucks)	Goods/Minerals (tons)	
Between stations on Speyside	139	2,040	£458
Beyond Craigellachie	576	54,729	£6,328
Beyond Boat of Garten	108	4,464	£659
Through between Craigellachie and Boat of Garten	29	4,729	£420
Total	**852**	**65,962**	**£7,865**
Deduct cartage			£253
			£7,612
Total (mails not included)			**£12,965**

Operating expenses

Traffic Department	£2,808
Locomotive Department	£3,117
Permanent Way Department	£1,882
Other charges	£2,313
Total	**£10,120**
Operating surplus	**£2,845**

1938   **London & North Eastern Railway**

Passengers

Station	Tickets	Income
Aberlour	6,386	£730
Carron	3,616	£241
Knockando	3,852	£338
Blacksboat	1,503	£151
Ballindalloch	1,598	£252
Advie	1,094	£155
Cromdale	928	£118
Grantown	1,613	£425
Nethy Bridge	1,639	£299
Boat of Garten	1,042	£189
Totals	**23,271**	**£2,898**

Merchandise/Minerals, Coal and Livestock

Stations	Merchandise & Minerals (tons)		Coal (tons)	Livestock (trucks)	
	In	Out	In	In	Out
Aberlour	3,431	3,477	4,344	92	11
Carron	5,352	2,935	3,316	7	5
Knockando	3,452	1,595	2,304	45	26
Ballindalloch & Blacksboat	5,231	4,781	5,287	78	189
Advie	483	46	127	32	51
Cromdale	2,972	1,262	1,806	29	39
Grantown	1,083	919	1,999	18	61
Nethy Bridge	1,065	77	756	9	13
Boat of Garten	815	10	26	3	11
Totals	**23,884**	**15,102**	**19,965**	**313**	**406**

Appendix 3 : Financial Performance of the Strathspey line

Source : GNSR papers.

Year ended 31st July 1869

Station expenses	£885
Maintenance	£965
Locomotives and guards	£845
10% on plant for interest and repairs	£500
Feu duties, rates and taxes	£450
Total (a)	**£3,645**
Gross Revenue from branch	£4,420
Gross Revenue drawn on main line (a)	£1,610
Total Gross Revenue	**£6,030**
Net Revenue	**£2,385**
Interest on unproductive capital invested by GNSR in branch @ 5%	£12,510
Less Net Revenue	£2,385
Loss on branch	£10,125
Capital cost of railway	£250,000
Average return on capital	0.95%

No allowance made for Head Office charges.

(a) Derived from traffic exchanged with branch less 30% for working expenses.

Year Ended 31st July 1903

Gross Revenue	£12,965
Traffic expenses	£2,808
Locomotive department	£3,117
Permanent way costs	£1,882
Feu duties, taxes, etc	£1,162
Other charges, including Head Office	£1,150
Total	**£10,119**
Net Revenue	**£2,846**
Capital cost : Railway	£300,000
Plant (a)	£14,291
Total	**£314,291**
Average percentage interest on capital (b)	0.91%

(a) Assumed that 2½ locomotives, 10 carriages and 50 wagons were required to work the line.

(b) At this time the average return on the Company's shares was about 2.1%.

Bibliography

Great North of Scotland Railway Minute Books and Papers

Speyside Railway Minute Books and Papers

Highland Railway Minute Books

Morayshire Railway Minute Books

Inverness & Aberdeen Junction Railway Minute Books

LNER papers

Board of Trade Inspection Reports

Great North Review, various issues including No.155, November 2002, Introduction to Classic Malts; No.181, May 2009, Sputnik on Speyside.

Great North of Scotland Railway - A Guide, W Ferguson of Kinmundy, *David Douglas (1881)*

Great North of Scotland Railway (2nd Edition), H A Vallance, *David St.John Thomas (1989)*

History of the Great North of Scotland Railway, Sir C M Barclay-Harvey, *Ian Allan.*

Regional History of the Railways of Great Britain, Vol.15, J Thomas & D Turnock, *David St.John Thomas (1989)*

Speyside Railways, Rosemary Burgess & Robert Kinghorn, *Aberdeen University Press (1988)*

Industrial Locomotives of Scotland, Industrial Railway Society (1976)

The Aviemore Line : Railway Politics in the Highlands 1882-98, N T Sinclair, *Transport History Vol32 No.3 (November 1969)*

Elgin Courant

Web Sites

Speyside Way : www.moray.gov.uk/area/speyway/webpages/swhome.htm

Strathspey Steam Railway : www.strathspeyrailway.co.uk/

Keith & Duffown Railway : www.keith-dufftown-railway.co.uk

The end of the line. The last train to Aviemore in November 1968 passes Tullochgorum where the Highland line was joined and GNSR ownership ended. By that time, the line to Forres had been closed for 3 years, although the track remained in situ.   *(Keith Fenwick)*

Great North of Scotland Railway Association

The Association caters for all those interested in the history of the Great North of Scotland Railway and its constituent companies, as well as the lines during the LNER, British Railways and post-privatisation periods. The Association promotes the study and collection of information, documents and illustrations relating to all aspects of the North East's railways. It also facilitates and co-ordinates members' research and provides information for modellers.

Members receive a quarterly *Review* containing articles, photographs, drawings and news of the railway, both historical and current. The Association has produced a comprehensive range of books and technical papers covering aspects of the railway in great detail. Members have access to an extensive photographic and drawing archive. Members receive a discount on Association publication. Meetings and excursions are regularly organised for the benefit of members.

For further information, please look at the Association's website www.gnsra.org.uk.